Mometrix
TEST PREPARATION

AEPA®

Dance (48) Secrets Study Guide

DEAR FUTURE EXAM SUCCESS STORY

First of all, **THANK YOU** for purchasing Mometrix study materials!

Second, congratulations! You are one of the few determined test-takers who are committed to doing whatever it takes to excel on your exam. **You have come to the right place.** We developed these study materials with one goal in mind: to deliver you the information you need in a format that's concise and easy to use.

In addition to optimizing your guide for the content of the test, we've outlined our recommended steps for breaking down the preparation process into small, attainable goals so you can make sure you stay on track.

We've also analyzed the entire test-taking process, identifying the most common pitfalls and showing how you can overcome them and be ready for any curveball the test throws you.

Standardized testing is one of the biggest obstacles on your road to success, which only increases the importance of doing well in the high-pressure, high-stakes environment of test day. Your results on this test could have a significant impact on your future, and this guide provides the information and practical advice to help you achieve your full potential on test day.

Your success is our success

We would love to hear from you! If you would like to share the story of your exam success or if you have any questions or comments in regard to our products, please contact us at **800-673-8175** or **support@mometrix.com**.

Thanks again for your business and we wish you continued success!

Sincerely,
The Mometrix Test Preparation Team

Need more help? Check out our flashcards at:
http://MometrixFlashcards.com/AEPA

TABLE OF CONTENTS

INTRODUCTION — 1
SECRET KEY #1 – PLAN BIG, STUDY SMALL — 2
SECRET KEY #2 – MAKE YOUR STUDYING COUNT — 3
SECRET KEY #3 – PRACTICE THE RIGHT WAY — 4
SECRET KEY #4 – PACE YOURSELF — 6
SECRET KEY #5 – HAVE A PLAN FOR GUESSING — 7
TEST-TAKING STRATEGIES — 10
DANCE ELEMENTS, CONCEPTS, AND SKILLS — 15
- MOVEMENT CONCEPTS & ANALYSIS — 15
- BALLET: CORE VOCABULARY & TECHNIQUE — 21
- MODERN DANCE: CORE VOCABULARY & TECHNIQUE — 24
- JAZZ & TAP: CORE VOCABULARY & TECHNIQUE — 27
- WORLD & SOCIAL DANCE: FORMS, VOCABULARY & PRACTICE — 31
- DANCER HEALTH, SAFETY & INJURY PREVENTION — 35
- CHAPTER QUIZ — 45

CREATING AND ANALYZING DANCE — 46
- CHOREOGRAPHIC IDEAS & PROCESSES — 46
- CHOREOGRAPHIC DEVICES, FORM & MUSICALITY — 52
- ANALYZING & EVALUATING DANCE WORKS — 58
- TEACHING TECHNIQUE, CREATIVITY & PERFORMANCE SKILLS — 64
- CHAPTER QUIZ — 69

THE HISTORY AND ROLES OF DANCE — 70
- DANCE IN CULTURAL CONTEXTS — 70
- GLOBAL HISTORY OF DANCE & INFLUENTIAL FIGURES — 73
- DANCE ACROSS THE ARTS & DISCIPLINES — 80
- CHAPTER QUIZ — 82

DANCE EDUCATION — 83
- KINESIOLOGY & SOMATICS FOR DANCERS — 83
- PRODUCTION ELEMENTS: TECH, ROLES & PERFORMANCE QUALITY — 90
- CURRICULUM DESIGN & INSTRUCTIONAL PLANNING IN DANCE — 99
- ASSESSMENT STRATEGIES IN DANCE EDUCATION — 103
- CHAPTER QUIZ — 109

AEPA PRACTICE TEST — 110
ANSWER KEY AND EXPLANATIONS — 126
HOW TO OVERCOME TEST ANXIETY — 138
ONLINE RESOURCES — 144

Introduction

Thank you for purchasing this resource! You have made the choice to prepare yourself for a test that could have a huge impact on your future, and this guide is designed to help you be fully ready for test day. Obviously, it's important to have a solid understanding of the test material, but you also need to be prepared for the unique environment and stressors of the test, so that you can perform to the best of your abilities.

For this purpose, the first section that appears in this guide is the **Secret Keys**. We've devoted countless hours to meticulously researching what works and what doesn't, and we've boiled down our findings to the five most impactful steps you can take to improve your performance on the test. We start at the beginning with study planning and move through the preparation process, all the way to the testing strategies that will help you get the most out of what you know when you're finally sitting in front of the test.

We recommend that you start preparing for your test as far in advance as possible. However, if you've bought this guide as a last-minute study resource and only have a few days before your test, we recommend that you skip over the first two Secret Keys since they address a long-term study plan.

If you struggle with **test anxiety**, we strongly encourage you to check out our recommendations for how you can overcome it. Test anxiety is a formidable foe, but it can be beaten, and we want to make sure you have the tools you need to defeat it.

Secret Key #1 – Plan Big, Study Small

There's a lot riding on your performance. If you want to ace this test, you're going to need to keep your skills sharp and the material fresh in your mind. You need a plan that lets you review everything you need to know while still fitting in your schedule. We'll break this strategy down into three categories.

Information Organization

Start with the information you already have: the official test outline. From this, you can make a complete list of all the concepts you need to cover before the test. Organize these concepts into groups that can be studied together, and create a list of any related vocabulary you need to learn so you can brush up on any difficult terms. You'll want to keep this vocabulary list handy once you actually start studying since you may need to add to it along the way.

Time Management

Once you have your set of study concepts, decide how to spread them out over the time you have left before the test. Break your study plan into small, clear goals so you have a manageable task for each day and know exactly what you're doing. Then just focus on one small step at a time. When you manage your time this way, you don't need to spend hours at a time studying. Studying a small block of content for a short period each day helps you retain information better and avoid stressing over how much you have left to do. You can relax knowing that you have a plan to cover everything in time. In order for this strategy to be effective though, you have to start studying early and stick to your schedule. Avoid the exhaustion and futility that comes from last-minute cramming!

Study Environment

The environment you study in has a big impact on your learning. Studying in a coffee shop, while probably more enjoyable, is not likely to be as fruitful as studying in a quiet room. It's important to keep distractions to a minimum. You're only planning to study for a short block of time, so make the most of it. Don't pause to check your phone or get up to find a snack. It's also important to **avoid multitasking**. Research has consistently shown that multitasking will make your studying dramatically less effective. Your study area should also be comfortable and well-lit so you don't have the distraction of straining your eyes or sitting on an uncomfortable chair.

The time of day you study is also important. You want to be rested and alert. Don't wait until just before bedtime. Study when you'll be most likely to comprehend and remember. Even better, if you know what time of day your test will be, set that time aside for study. That way your brain will be used to working on that subject at that specific time and you'll have a better chance of recalling information.

Finally, it can be helpful to team up with others who are studying for the same test. Your actual studying should be done in as isolated an environment as possible, but the work of organizing the information and setting up the study plan can be divided up. In between study sessions, you can discuss with your teammates the concepts that you're all studying and quiz each other on the details. Just be sure that your teammates are as serious about the test as you are. If you find that your study time is being replaced with social time, you might need to find a new team.

Secret Key #2 – Make Your Studying Count

You're devoting a lot of time and effort to preparing for this test, so you want to be absolutely certain it will pay off. This means doing more than just reading the content and hoping you can remember it on test day. It's important to make every minute of study count. There are two main areas you can focus on to make your studying count.

Retention

It doesn't matter how much time you study if you can't remember the material. You need to make sure you are retaining the concepts. To check your retention of the information you're learning, try recalling it at later times with minimal prompting. Try carrying around flashcards and glance at one or two from time to time or ask a friend who's also studying for the test to quiz you.

To enhance your retention, look for ways to put the information into practice so that you can apply it rather than simply recalling it. If you're using the information in practical ways, it will be much easier to remember. Similarly, it helps to solidify a concept in your mind if you're not only reading it to yourself but also explaining it to someone else. Ask a friend to let you teach them about a concept you're a little shaky on (or speak aloud to an imaginary audience if necessary). As you try to summarize, define, give examples, and answer your friend's questions, you'll understand the concepts better and they will stay with you longer. Finally, step back for a big picture view and ask yourself how each piece of information fits with the whole subject. When you link the different concepts together and see them working together as a whole, it's easier to remember the individual components.

Finally, practice showing your work on any multi-step problems, even if you're just studying. Writing out each step you take to solve a problem will help solidify the process in your mind, and you'll be more likely to remember it during the test.

Modality

Modality simply refers to the means or method by which you study. Choosing a study modality that fits your own individual learning style is crucial. No two people learn best in exactly the same way, so it's important to know your strengths and use them to your advantage.

For example, if you learn best by visualization, focus on visualizing a concept in your mind and draw an image or a diagram. Try color-coding your notes, illustrating them, or creating symbols that will trigger your mind to recall a learned concept. If you learn best by hearing or discussing information, find a study partner who learns the same way or read aloud to yourself. Think about how to put the information in your own words. Imagine that you are giving a lecture on the topic and record yourself so you can listen to it later.

For any learning style, flashcards can be helpful. Organize the information so you can take advantage of spare moments to review. Underline key words or phrases. Use different colors for different categories. Mnemonic devices (such as creating a short list in which every item starts with the same letter) can also help with retention. Find what works best for you and use it to store the information in your mind most effectively and easily.

Secret Key #3 – Practice the Right Way

Your success on test day depends not only on how many hours you put into preparing, but also on whether you prepared the right way. It's good to check along the way to see if your studying is paying off. One of the most effective ways to do this is by taking practice tests to evaluate your progress. Practice tests are useful because they show exactly where you need to improve. Every time you take a practice test, pay special attention to these three groups of questions:

- The questions you got wrong
- The questions you had to guess on, even if you guessed right
- The questions you found difficult or slow to work through

This will show you exactly what your weak areas are, and where you need to devote more study time. Ask yourself why each of these questions gave you trouble. Was it because you didn't understand the material? Was it because you didn't remember the vocabulary? Do you need more repetitions on this type of question to build speed and confidence? Dig into those questions and figure out how you can strengthen your weak areas as you go back to review the material.

Additionally, many practice tests have a section explaining the answer choices. It can be tempting to read the explanation and think that you now have a good understanding of the concept. However, an explanation likely only covers part of the question's broader context. Even if the explanation makes perfect sense, **go back and investigate** every concept related to the question until you're positive you have a thorough understanding.

As you go along, keep in mind that the practice test is just that: practice. Memorizing these questions and answers will not be very helpful on the actual test because it is unlikely to have any of the same exact questions. If you only know the right answers to the sample questions, you won't be prepared for the real thing. **Study the concepts** until you understand them fully, and then you'll be able to answer any question that shows up on the test.

It's important to wait on the practice tests until you're ready. If you take a test on your first day of study, you may be overwhelmed by the amount of material covered and how much you need to learn. Work up to it gradually.

On test day, you'll need to be prepared for answering questions, managing your time, and using the test-taking strategies you've learned. It's a lot to balance, like a mental marathon that will have a big impact on your future. Like training for a marathon, you'll need to start slowly and work your way up. When test day arrives, you'll be ready.

Start with the strategies you've read in the first two Secret Keys—plan your course and study in the way that works best for you. If you have time, consider using multiple study resources to get different approaches to the same concepts. It can be helpful to see difficult concepts from more than one angle. Then find a good source for practice tests. Many times, the test website will suggest potential study resources or provide sample tests.

Practice Test Strategy

If you're able to find at least three practice tests, we recommend this strategy:

Untimed and Open-Book Practice

Take the first test with no time constraints and with your notes and study guide handy. Take your time and focus on applying the strategies you've learned.

Timed and Open-Book Practice

Take the second practice test open-book as well, but set a timer and practice pacing yourself to finish in time.

Timed and Closed-Book Practice

Take any other practice tests as if it were test day. Set a timer and put away your study materials. Sit at a table or desk in a quiet room, imagine yourself at the testing center, and answer questions as quickly and accurately as possible.

Keep repeating timed and closed-book tests on a regular basis until you run out of practice tests or it's time for the actual test. Your mind will be ready for the schedule and stress of test day, and you'll be able to focus on recalling the material you've learned.

Secret Key #4 – Pace Yourself

Once you're fully prepared for the material on the test, your biggest challenge on test day will be managing your time. Just knowing that the clock is ticking can make you panic even if you have plenty of time left. Work on pacing yourself so you can build confidence against the time constraints of the exam. Pacing is a difficult skill to master, especially in a high-pressure environment, so **practice is vital**.

Set time expectations for your pace based on how much time is available. For example, if a section has 60 questions and the time limit is 30 minutes, you know you have to average 30 seconds or less per question in order to answer them all. Although 30 seconds is the hard limit, set 25 seconds per question as your goal, so you reserve extra time to spend on harder questions. When you budget extra time for the harder questions, you no longer have any reason to stress when those questions take longer to answer.

Don't let this time expectation distract you from working through the test at a calm, steady pace, but keep it in mind so you don't spend too much time on any one question. Recognize that taking extra time on one question you don't understand may keep you from answering two that you do understand later in the test. If your time limit for a question is up and you're still not sure of the answer, mark it and move on, and come back to it later if the time and the test format allow. If the testing format doesn't allow you to return to earlier questions, just make an educated guess; then put it out of your mind and move on.

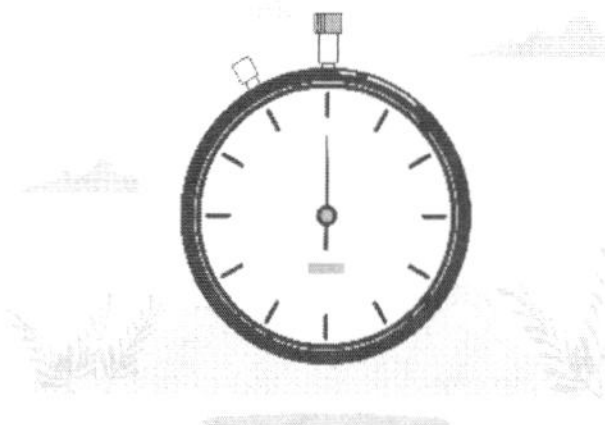

On the easier questions, be careful not to rush. It may seem wise to hurry through them so you have more time for the challenging ones, but it's not worth missing one if you know the concept and just didn't take the time to read the question fully. Work efficiently but make sure you understand the question and have looked at all of the answer choices, since more than one may seem right at first.

Even if you're paying attention to the time, you may find yourself a little behind at some point. You should speed up to get back on track, but do so wisely. Don't panic; just take a few seconds less on each question until you're caught up. Don't guess without thinking, but do look through the answer choices and eliminate any you know are wrong. If you can get down to two choices, it is often worthwhile to guess from those. Once you've chosen an answer, move on and don't dwell on any that you skipped or had to hurry through. If a question was taking too long, chances are it was one of the harder ones, so you weren't as likely to get it right anyway.

On the other hand, if you find yourself getting ahead of schedule, it may be beneficial to slow down a little. The more quickly you work, the more likely you are to make a careless mistake that will affect your score. You've budgeted time for each question, so don't be afraid to spend that time. Practice an efficient but careful pace to get the most out of the time you have.

Secret Key #5 – Have a Plan for Guessing

When you're taking the test, you may find yourself stuck on a question. Some of the answer choices seem better than others, but you don't see the one answer choice that is obviously correct. What do you do?

The scenario described above is very common, yet most test takers have not effectively prepared for it. Developing and practicing a plan for guessing may be one of the single most effective uses of your time as you get ready for the exam.

In developing your plan for guessing, there are three questions to address:

- When should you start the guessing process?
- How should you narrow down the choices?
- Which answer should you choose?

When to Start the Guessing Process

Unless your plan for guessing is to select C every time (which, despite its merits, is not what we recommend), you need to leave yourself enough time to apply your answer elimination strategies. Since you have a limited amount of time for each question, that means that if you're going to give yourself the best shot at guessing correctly, you have to decide quickly whether or not you will guess.

Of course, the best-case scenario is that you don't have to guess at all, so first, see if you can answer the question based on your knowledge of the subject and basic reasoning skills. Focus on the key words in the question and try to jog your memory of related topics. Give yourself a chance to bring the knowledge to mind, but once you realize that you don't have (or you can't access) the knowledge you need to answer the question, it's time to start the guessing process.

It's almost always better to start the guessing process too early than too late. It only takes a few seconds to remember something and answer the question from knowledge. Carefully eliminating wrong answer choices takes longer. Plus, going through the process of eliminating answer choices can actually help jog your memory.

Summary: Start the guessing process as soon as you decide that you can't answer the question based on your knowledge.

How to Narrow Down the Choices

The next chapter in this book (**Test-Taking Strategies**) includes a wide range of strategies for how to approach questions and how to look for answer choices to eliminate. You will definitely want to read those carefully, practice them, and figure out which ones work best for you. Here though, we're going to address a mindset rather than a particular strategy.

Your odds of guessing an answer correctly depend on how many options you are choosing from.

Number of options left	5	4	3	2	1
Odds of guessing correctly	20%	25%	33%	50%	100%

You can see from this chart just how valuable it is to be able to eliminate incorrect answers and make an educated guess, but there are two things that many test takers do that cause them to miss out on the benefits of guessing:

- Accidentally eliminating the correct answer
- Selecting an answer based on an impression

We'll look at the first one here, and the second one in the next section.

To avoid accidentally eliminating the correct answer, we recommend a thought exercise called **the $5 challenge**. In this challenge, you only eliminate an answer choice from contention if you are willing to bet $5 on it being wrong. Why $5? Five dollars is a small but not insignificant amount of money. It's an amount you could afford to lose but wouldn't want to throw away. And while losing $5 once might not hurt too much, doing it twenty times will set you back $100. In the same way, each small decision you make—eliminating a choice here, guessing on a question there—won't by itself impact your score very much, but when you put them all together, they can make a big difference. By holding each answer choice elimination decision to a higher standard, you can reduce the risk of accidentally eliminating the correct answer.

The $5 challenge can also be applied in a positive sense: If you are willing to bet $5 that an answer choice *is* correct, go ahead and mark it as correct.

Summary: Only eliminate an answer choice if you are willing to bet $5 that it is wrong.

Which Answer to Choose

You're taking the test. You've run into a hard question and decided you'll have to guess. You've eliminated all the answer choices you're willing to bet $5 on. Now you have to pick an answer. Why do we even need to talk about this? Why can't you just pick whichever one you feel like when the time comes?

The answer to these questions is that if you don't come into the test with a plan, you'll rely on your impression to select an answer choice, and if you do that, you risk falling into a trap. The test writers know that everyone who takes their test will be guessing on some of the questions, so they intentionally write wrong answer choices to seem plausible. You still have to pick an answer though, and if the wrong answer choices are designed to look right, how can you ever be sure that you're not falling for their trap? The best solution we've found to this dilemma is to take the decision out of your hands entirely. Here is the process we recommend:

Once you've eliminated any choices that you are confident (willing to bet $5) are wrong, select the first remaining choice as your answer.

Whether you choose to select the first remaining choice, the second, or the last, the important thing is that you use some preselected standard. Using this approach guarantees that you will not be enticed into selecting an answer choice that looks right, because you are not basing your decision on how the answer choices look.

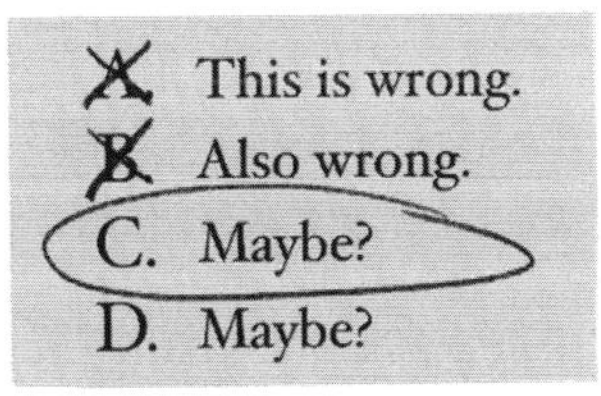

This is not meant to make you question your knowledge. Instead, it is to help you recognize the difference between your knowledge and your impressions. There's a huge difference between thinking an answer is right because of what you know, and thinking an answer is right because it looks or sounds like it should be right.

Summary: To ensure that your selection is appropriately random, make a predetermined selection from among all answer choices you have not eliminated.

Test-Taking Strategies

This section contains a list of test-taking strategies that you may find helpful as you work through the test. By taking what you know and applying logical thought, you can maximize your chances of answering any question correctly!

It is very important to realize that every question is different and every person is different: no single strategy will work on every question, and no single strategy will work for every person. That's why we've included all of them here, so you can try them out and determine which ones work best for different types of questions and which ones work best for you.

Question Strategies

⊘ Read Carefully

Read the question and the answer choices carefully. Don't miss the question because you misread the terms. You have plenty of time to read each question thoroughly and make sure you understand what is being asked. Yet a happy medium must be attained, so don't waste too much time. You must read carefully and efficiently.

⊘ Contextual Clues

Look for contextual clues. If the question includes a word you are not familiar with, look at the immediate context for some indication of what the word might mean. Contextual clues can often give you all the information you need to decipher the meaning of an unfamiliar word. Even if you can't determine the meaning, you may be able to narrow down the possibilities enough to make a solid guess at the answer to the question.

⊘ Prefixes

If you're having trouble with a word in the question or answer choices, try dissecting it. Take advantage of every clue that the word might include. Prefixes can be a huge help. Usually, they allow you to determine a basic meaning. *Pre-* means before, *post-* means after, *pro-* is positive, *de-* is negative. From prefixes, you can get an idea of the general meaning of the word and try to put it into context.

⊘ Hedge Words

Watch out for critical hedge words, such as *likely, may, can, often, almost, mostly, usually, generally, rarely*, and *sometimes*. Question writers insert these hedge phrases to cover every possibility. Often an answer choice will be wrong simply because it leaves no room for exception. Be on guard for answer choices that have definitive words such as *exactly* and *always*.

⊘ Switchback Words

Stay alert for *switchbacks*. These are the words and phrases frequently used to alert you to shifts in thought. The most common switchback words are *but, although*, and *however*. Others include *nevertheless, on the other hand, even though, while, in spite of, despite*, and *regardless of*. Switchback words are important to catch because they can change the direction of the question or an answer choice.

☑ FACE VALUE

When in doubt, use common sense. Accept the situation in the problem at face value. Don't read too much into it. These problems will not require you to make wild assumptions. If you have to go beyond creativity and warp time or space in order to have an answer choice fit the question, then you should move on and consider the other answer choices. These are normal problems rooted in reality. The applicable relationship or explanation may not be readily apparent, but it is there for you to figure out. Use your common sense to interpret anything that isn't clear.

Answer Choice Strategies

☑ ANSWER SELECTION

The most thorough way to pick an answer choice is to identify and eliminate wrong answers until only one is left, then confirm it is the correct answer. Sometimes an answer choice may immediately seem right, but be careful. The test writers will usually put more than one reasonable answer choice on each question, so take a second to read all of them and make sure that the other choices are not equally obvious. As long as you have time left, it is better to read every answer choice than to pick the first one that looks right without checking the others.

☑ ANSWER CHOICE FAMILIES

An answer choice family consists of two (in rare cases, three) answer choices that are very similar in construction and cannot all be true at the same time. If you see two answer choices that are direct opposites or parallels, one of them is usually the correct answer. For instance, if one answer choice says that quantity *x* increases and another either says that quantity *x* decreases (opposite) or says that quantity *y* increases (parallel), then those answer choices would fall into the same family. An answer choice that doesn't match the construction of the answer choice family is more likely to be incorrect. Most questions will not have answer choice families, but when they do appear, you should be prepared to recognize them.

☑ ELIMINATE ANSWERS

Eliminate answer choices as soon as you realize they are wrong, but make sure you consider all possibilities. If you are eliminating answer choices and realize that the last one you are left with is also wrong, don't panic. Start over and consider each choice again. There may be something you missed the first time that you will realize on the second pass.

☑ AVOID FACT TRAPS

Don't be distracted by an answer choice that is factually true but doesn't answer the question. You are looking for the choice that answers the question. Stay focused on what the question is asking for so you don't accidentally pick an answer that is true but incorrect. Always go back to the question and make sure the answer choice you've selected actually answers the question and is not merely a true statement.

☑ EXTREME STATEMENTS

In general, you should avoid answers that put forth extreme actions as standard practice or proclaim controversial ideas as established fact. An answer choice that states the "process should be used in certain situations, if..." is much more likely to be correct than one that states the "process should be discontinued completely." The first is a calm rational statement and doesn't even make a definitive, uncompromising stance, using a hedge word *if* to provide wiggle room, whereas the second choice is far more extreme.

⊘ Benchmark

As you read through the answer choices and you come across one that seems to answer the question well, mentally select that answer choice. This is not your final answer, but it's the one that will help you evaluate the other answer choices. The one that you selected is your benchmark or standard for judging each of the other answer choices. Every other answer choice must be compared to your benchmark. That choice is correct until proven otherwise by another answer choice beating it. If you find a better answer, then that one becomes your new benchmark. Once you've decided that no other choice answers the question as well as your benchmark, you have your final answer.

⊘ Predict the Answer

Before you even start looking at the answer choices, it is often best to try to predict the answer. When you come up with the answer on your own, it is easier to avoid distractions and traps because you will know exactly what to look for. The right answer choice is unlikely to be word-for-word what you came up with, but it should be a close match. Even if you are confident that you have the right answer, you should still take the time to read each option before moving on.

General Strategies

⊘ Tough Questions

If you are stumped on a problem or it appears too hard or too difficult, don't waste time. Move on! Remember though, if you can quickly check for obviously incorrect answer choices, your chances of guessing correctly are greatly improved. Before you completely give up, at least try to knock out a couple of possible answers. Eliminate what you can and then guess at the remaining answer choices before moving on.

⊘ Check Your Work

Since you will probably not know every term listed and the answer to every question, it is important that you get credit for the ones that you do know. Don't miss any questions through careless mistakes. If at all possible, try to take a second to look back over your answer selection and make sure you've selected the correct answer choice and haven't made a costly careless mistake (such as marking an answer choice that you didn't mean to mark). This quick double check should more than pay for itself in caught mistakes for the time it costs.

⊘ Pace Yourself

It's easy to be overwhelmed when you're looking at a page full of questions; your mind is confused and full of random thoughts, and the clock is ticking down faster than you would like. Calm down and maintain the pace that you have set for yourself. Especially as you get down to the last few minutes of the test, don't let the small numbers on the clock make you panic. As long as you are on track by monitoring your pace, you are guaranteed to have time for each question.

⊘ Don't Rush

It is very easy to make errors when you are in a hurry. Maintaining a fast pace in answering questions is pointless if it makes you miss questions that you would have gotten right otherwise. Test writers like to include distracting information and wrong answers that seem right. Taking a little extra time to avoid careless mistakes can make all the difference in your test score. Find a pace that allows you to be confident in the answers that you select.

✓ KEEP MOVING

Panicking will not help you pass the test, so do your best to stay calm and keep moving. Taking deep breaths and going through the answer elimination steps you practiced can help to break through a stress barrier and keep your pace.

Final Notes

The combination of a solid foundation of content knowledge and the confidence that comes from practicing your plan for applying that knowledge is the key to maximizing your performance on test day. As your foundation of content knowledge is built up and strengthened, you'll find that the strategies included in this chapter become more and more effective in helping you quickly sift through the distractions and traps of the test to isolate the correct answer.

Now that you're preparing to move forward into the test content chapters of this book, be sure to keep your goal in mind. As you read, think about how you will be able to apply this information on the test. If you've already seen sample questions for the test and you have an idea of the question format and style, try to come up with questions of your own that you can answer based on what you're reading. This will give you valuable practice applying your knowledge in the same ways you can expect to on test day.

Good luck and good studying!

Dance Elements, Concepts, and Skills

Movement Concepts & Analysis

Gravity

Gravity is a constant physical force that affects human movement. It defines for us the concept of vertical, as it pulls any object or body toward the earth vertically from its point(s) of support. While movement can only be achieved by musculature working to counteract gravity, the human body also works to resist gravity when it is still. Thus, resisting gravity allows the body both to move and to maintain positions over time.

Dancers learn to move both with gravity and against it to achieve various movement objectives. In the contexts of falling and swinging and even rolling, a dancer cooperates with the force of gravity for the downward portion of the movement. Conversely, the lifting of any appendage or limb, or even the entire body—either in partnered lifts or in leaps and jumps—requires work to counteract gravity, as does the maintaining of a position in a balance.

Energy in the Context of Movement Analysis

- **Energy** → Energy is the animating factor that overcomes stasis or gravity to initiate or affect movement in a body. When creating movement, energy is applied over time and in space to become force.
- **Force** → Force is the amount of energy applied in a movement, and ranges in intensity from gentle to strong.
- **Dynamics** → Dynamics is the interaction of force and time, which results in movement that imparts an impression to the viewer; as a movement's dynamics vary, the resulting impression varies. The term is often used interchangeably with movement quality, but connotes a more theoretical context.
- **Movement Quality** → Movement quality refers to the traits created by the application of energy in a body, which results in movement executed in a particular way. Movement qualities are often evoked by words and images describing the forces of time, space, energy, weight, and flow. These forces act upon the movement in various combinations, which range from simple to complex.

Factors that Contribute to Effort

- **Time** → Time refers to the length of time a movement takes, from initiation to completion. It is described on a continuum. The extremes of this continuum are "quick" (sometimes also characterized as "sudden") and "sustained."
- **Space** → Space is the intentional quality of the path taken by a body part or a body through space during a movement. The two polarities of space are "direct" and "indirect."
- **Weight** → Weight is the degree of the force (the impact) of body weight introduced into a movement. The two polarities of weight are "strong" and "light."
- **Flow** → Flow is the degree of ease or continuousness of a movement from initiation to completion, or during the transition into the next movement. The two polarities of flow are "bound" and "free."

Interactions between the first three factors result in eight main movement descriptors that Laban Movement Analysis calls the Effort Actions. These are: float, punch (also called "thrust"), glide, slash, dab, wring, flick, and press.

Effort Actions Described by Laban Movement Analysis

- **Float** → Combination: sustained time/indirect space/light weight
  - Illustrative Image: the easy action of a down feather sailing on a light breeze
- **Punch** → Combination: sudden time/direct space/strong weight
  - Illustrative Image: a heavy fist suddenly thrown at a boxing opponent
- **Glide** → Combination: sustained time/direct space/light weight
  - Illustrative Image: the smooth action of a skier skiing down a hill
- **Slash** → Combination: sudden time/indirect space/strong weight
  - Illustrative Image: a combative sweeping blow with a switchblade
- **Dab** → Combination: sudden time/direct space/light weight
  - Illustrative Image: the gentle application of dots of makeup onto a face
- **Wring** → Combination: sustained time/indirect space/strong weight
  - Illustrative Image: the intense grinding of spice in a mortar and pestle
- **Flick** → Combination: sudden time/indirect space/light weight
  - Illustrative Image: a quick, attention-getting tap on the shoulder
- **Press** → Combination: sustained time/direct space/strong weight
  - Illustrative Image: the effortful action of pushing a stalled car

Movement Quality

Movement qualities can be defined as the forces that act upon the execution of any given movement. These forces include time, space, weight, and flow. These forces interact in endless combinations to shape gestures or movements, which communicate different impressions depending on the combination of their makeup. The clearer a choreographer's/dancer's understanding of movement qualities during the creation, manipulation, or performance of a movement, the clearer the intent and effect of the movement will likely be.

Single, descriptive words can be used to evoke images that convey several aspects of movement quality or effort simultaneously. For example, the words "floating" and "airy" give a sense of a movement's time (sustained, probably slow), space (indirect), weight (light), and flow (free). On the other end of the effort/weight spectrum, words like "dragging" and "dense" can convey a sense of heavy and bound, but still slow, movement.

Flow

Flow is associated with the quality of continuity, the momentum (or lack thereof) within a single movement or in a transition between movements. Flow often invests movement with its vitality and expressiveness, as it so clearly communicates emotion and mental state through the degree to which a dancer visibly releases or contains the energy of a movement.

The two polarities of flow are "bound" and "free." **Free flow** is continuous and unbroken; thus, it can communicate images of ease, fluidity, freedom, joy, outpouring, and release. It is also associated with modes of locomotion, as in movements that recall flying, sailing, running, or rolling. **Bound flow** is characterized by the stopping of motion with varying degrees of intensity. It can communicate images of halting, containment, constraint, suppression, control, and worry. Bound flow at its furthest edge contributes to stillness and balance.

Levels of Movement in Dance

The **low level** connotes downward movement, on and into the floor. It facilitates positions and actions such as lying, crouching, sitting, kneeling, rolling, crawling, scooting, dragging, etc. Low is associated with all things grounded/heavy/earthy, sometimes with dirty/base/ugly/evil or even subhuman things, and sometimes with disadvantage/poverty/sadness/dejection.

The **middle level** is the "human" level. It facilitates level movement and positions and actions such as standing (in plié, on flat, or on relevé), walking, running, and skipping. This level is associated with human/pedestrian/mundane ideas, humility and regularity, and locomotion and transition. It can also carry neutral connotations, as it is the plane on which most humans operate daily.

The **high level** carries connotations of upward movement, air, ether, elevation, and flying. It facilitates actions such as lifting, leaping, and jumping, and evokes images of soaring and sailing. It is associated with things that are heavenly/holy, remote/unattainable, weightless/timeless/effortless, and sometimes superhuman.

Planes of Action Demonstrated in Human Movement

The **frontal plane** (also known as lateral or vertical) can be visualized as running vertically across the chest, shoulder to shoulder, on an upright standing body. Movement analyst Rudolf Laban characterized this as "the door plane." It can be understood as the combination of the dimensions of height and width. Basic movements of adduction and abduction occur on the lateral plane.

The **sagittal plane** runs vertically from the front to the back of an upright standing body, from the nose to the back of the head, for instance. Laban called this "the wheel plane." It can be understood as the dimensional combination of depth and height. Movements of flexion, extension, and hyperextension occur on the sagittal plane.

The **transverse plane** (horizontal) intersects an upright standing body horizontally, parallel to the ground. Laban called this "the table plane." It can be understood as the dimensional combination of width and depth. Rotational movements occur on the transverse plane.

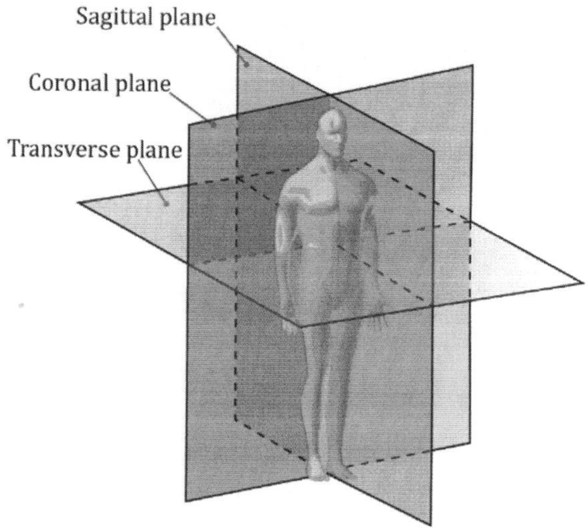

Aspects of Space That Are Commonly Manipulated to Develop Choreography

- **Shape** → Dancing bodies create shapes, which can be categorized as curved/straight, as symmetrical/asymmetrical, and in terms of negative/positive space. Movements also trace shapes in space. These shapes are called spatial paths
- **Dimension/Plane** → The three planes of human movement are: lateral/frontal plane, running vertically from shoulder to shoulder; sagittal plane, running vertically from front to back; and transverse plane, running horizontally, parallel to the ground
- **Level** → There are three levels of movement. Low level allows downward movement, on or into the floor. Middle level facilitates pedestrian locomotion on "the human plane." High level allows jumping, leaping, and lifting into the air
- **Staging/Floor Patterns/Facing/Direction** → Creating staging involves making choices about how the performance space should be used. Floor patterns are movement paths traced along the floor. Facings are the downstage, upstage, stage left, and stage right directions where movement can be focused. Directions are the paths along which dancers move from spot to spot on the stage

Shape

Statically, shape describes the design a body makes in space, or the collective shape made by a group of bodies. Dynamically, shape can also refer to the path a movement creates from its initiation to completion.

The shape made by a body can be **symmetrical**, with the limbs on each lateral side of the body in the same "matching" position, or **asymmetrical**, with each side's limbs in different positions. Either state can also be achieved by multiple bodies. Symmetrical shapes can be made by dancers "mirroring" each other, either facing each other in opposition, or facing the same direction in succession. Symmetrical shapes give an impression of stability, balance, and control, while asymmetry connotes variety, movement, and dynamism.

Shape is also described by whether the lines are curved or straight. Straight lines give an air of stasis and rigidity, while curved lines imply flow, resiliency, and softness.

Dynamic Shape

The shape of a movement from initiation to completion—the pattern it traces in space—is called a **spatial path**. This is a more abstract conception of shape, as a path is ever-changing and never overtly visible. A path can involve the body as a whole, or it can feature several paths, as each body part contributes to the choreography. For example, the pattern made by the left hand will create a different path than the one made by the right knee.

The shape along which a dancer travels on the floor during a dance is also called a **path**. Like other shapes, floor paths give different impressions based on their configuration and placement within the whole design. Straight lines are direct, curves are flowing and indirect, zigzags and angles are jarring, spirals are hypnotic, and circles are powerful and exclusive or inclusive.

Spatial Tension

Spatial tension is the arrangement of solid elements—body parts, dancers, and even props or other objects—in such a way that the space between them becomes noticeable. For example, Martha Graham achieved visible spatial tension in shapes she made onstage by wearing long skirts that stretched across her knees during every plié, drawing attention to the line of connection between them. When spatial tension is achieved by careful placement of bodies or objects in the field of human perception, perspective and focus are also involved in perceiving the negative space.

Positive space is filled up by a tangible form; negative space is the **empty space** around the form. When shapes in the positive space are arranged carefully, it can give shape to the negative space. This is what the eye notices in spatial tension, shifting a viewer's focus to the connection rather than the objects being connected.

Kinesphere

Kinesphere is sometimes called "reach space" or "personal space," and can be described as the entire area within a stationary human body's (and its limbs) reach. The kinesphere travels with the dancer at all times, changing its form as the limbs, spine, and head move the body into different shapes.

The kinesphere is associated with postural (or whole-body) movement, which happens solely within a dancer's personal space, as opposed to traveling and locomotion, which happens in and across the larger performance (or rehearsal) space.

Beat, Accent, and Meter

A **beat** is the main unit of rhythm—the repeating "strike" that provides animation to music and movement. Beats can be stressed (strong) or unstressed (weak), depending on the emphasis, or accent, placed upon them. Rhythmic patterns are created by combinations of strong and weak beats. **Accenting** a particular beat at a repeating interval creates **meter**, or the grouping of beats in a piece of music. The meter of a waltz has three beats, with an accent placed on the first beat.

Many forms of dance, such as ballet and jazz, match movement to the meter of accompanying music to create a concordant impression. Both forms use the same tone and follow the same structure. Other dance forms, such as modern and tap, frequently choose either to match movement to the beat or to counter it. This is done to produce differing impressions, which the tone of the dance requires.

Humans are intimately familiar with **rhythm**—heartbeats, breaths, the rhythm of walking on two feet—and we respond to beats both consciously and unconsciously.

Rhythmic patterns can affect our impression of a dance. Steady, regular beats elicit feelings of comfort, safety, and order, and irregular ones elicit unease, a sense of unpredictability, and sometimes excitement.

Similarly, **tempo**—the speed at which music is played or movement is performed—can be regular or varied. Slower tempos convey restfulness, indolence, or trance, while faster ones convey haste, urgency, and stimulation.

Like tempo and rhythmic patterns, accents in rhythm can be matched or opposed, either with accompanying music or within the rhythm of the movement if there is no music. Placing movement accents counter to musical accents can serve to wake up, discomfit, galvanize, or annoy an audience, or to make them laugh.

Syncopation and Polyrhythm

Syncopation is placing an accent on a normally weak beat, or "between" beats. It can also refer to the absence of an accent on an expected strong beat. Because a listener's or viewer's attention is given to beats that are accented, the use of syncopation can serve to "spice up" a regular rhythm of music or movement. Syncopation is often used in tap dance and jazz, where there is a strong emphasis on improvisation and personal style.

The term polyrhythm refers to simple, multiple, and different rhythm patterns played at the same time. The layering of rhythms over each other can create sensations of gathering, complexity, urgency, overwhelming force, and even—ironically—unity. Developing a dance to polyrhythmic music can afford a choreographer the opportunity to create several movement motifs (and possibly characters) to correspond with each rhythm, to single out one rhythm or a few rhythms, or to ignore the rhythms completely. Each choice creates its own effect.

Imagery

The human brain comprehends and assimilates familiar images more readily than analytical information or technical instruction, especially in a quick-moving environment such as a dance class or a rehearsal, where dancers must continually adjust and "think on their feet." Additionally, since dance is an expressive form of movement which seeks to communicate meaning through physical images, it follows that making visual, kinesthetic, or emotional images part of the student's learning process will elicit more evocative and expressive movement from the student. Teachers can take advantage of the natural human affinity for mimicry, and can present students with images to mimic that will embody the qualities of the desired movement.

Imagery connects the unfamiliar with the familiar, allowing a dancer to understand and feel the movement being performed. Following are some examples of imagery that could be used to improve technique, and their desired effects.

- **To improve balance**: The image of sand slowly falling and accumulating (as in an hourglass) to fill up a standing leg
- **To prolong lift in a leap**: The image of a gazelle leaping and remaining suspended for a second before landing
- **To achieve deeper abdominal contraction**: The image of a snail curling deep into its spiraling shell

- **To sharpen angular movement and shapes**: The image of skyscrapers that are full of hard lines and acute angles
- **To soften tension in port de bras**: The image of a soft blanket gently gliding over the skin, or of gentle waves washing the arms
- **To accelerate attack in an assemblé**: The image of stepping on a dollar bill before someone else gets it
- **To better employ plié in preparation for jumps**: The image of a floor made out of springs

Achieving Proper Alignment

Mimicry comes naturally to humans from birth; it is how we learn to talk, move, and feed ourselves. This process for attaining skills and knowledge soon becomes instinctual. A dancer's natural response to an image is to "mimic" a physical representation of that image, resulting in movement that is evocative and organic.

For teachers helping dancers correct joint alignment and posture, one use of imagery may involve asking students to visualize the arches of the foot as a dome. Or, if a teacher is trying to help a student achieve elongated posture without excessive muscular tension, he or she may tell the dancer to "unfurl the spine from the pelvis like a vine growing up from a pot." Or, a teacher aiming for more fluidity in a dancer's thoracic spine may invoke the image of a lithe sapling swaying in the wind. Both images can result in more organic and successful responses than body-part-by-body-part instructions.

Ballet: Core Vocabulary & Technique

Language of Ballet

The progenitor of ballet was dance that originated during the Italian Renaissance. Grand spectacles of dance were performed for the amusement of royalty. When Catherine de Medici of the Italian ruling family later migrated to France in 1553 to marry Henry II, soon to become the king of France, she brought court musicians and dancers with her. Thus, the courtly but as-yet-uncodified dance form was established in France.

Over the next century and a half, ballet was not only embraced by the French, but also refined, expanded upon, systematized, and taught to succeeding generations. In 1661, King Louis XIV established the Royal Academy of Dance, which was the world's first professional ballet school. By 1700, much of the familiar French vocabulary for balletic movement was established. Around this time, other countries founded their own ballet schools and styles, most notably Russia, Denmark, and Italy, followed later by England and the United States.

Earliest Methods of Classical Ballet That Are Still Taught Today

The two methods to develop from the original French form of classical ballet are the Vaganova method from Russia and the Cecchetti method from Italy.

The **Russian (Vaganova) method** used today was developed in the late-19th century by Agrippina Vaganova, a graduate from the Russian Imperial Ballet School. This style focuses on lower back strength, flexibility, precise placement of the arms, endurance, and the lyrical qualities necessary for the classical pas de deux. It is also sometimes known for its dramatic qualities.

The **Italian (Cecchetti) method**, developed in Italy by Ballets Russes dancer Enrico Cecchetti in the mid-19th century, is a rigid procedure that exercises different muscles in a weekly sequence, imparting evenness of strength and flexibility. The style also focuses on an understanding of the connections between the limbs, torso, and head to create fluid lines as a cohesive whole, rather than pieces to be moved separately.

The **Royal Academy of Dance** (RAD), also known as The Royal Ballet, was founded in London in 1920, and has become the foundation for all ballet methods throughout the world. It combines aspects of the Italian, French, and Russian styles into one that balances rigorous technical training with an emphasis on elegance and fluidity.

The **French School of the Paris Opera Ballet** (l'École Française) focuses on elegance, fluidity, grace, and sophistication of gesture above technical virtuosity. It also trains dancers to perform numerous steps extremely quickly. These steps are performed so closely together that they give the impression of gliding.

The **Bournonville School** was developed by the director of the Royal Danish Ballet, August Bournonville, in the mid-19th century. Its early style closely followed the French method, but later integrated Russian elements to form its own distinct, romantic flavor, incorporating many quick beats within the footwork accompanied by very basic, graceful arm positioning.

Physical Characteristics and Movement Philosophies of Classical Ballet

Classical ballet technique revolves around a dancer's lifted, contracted torso. To provide stability, strength in the core muscles of the body is needed. The limbs are elevated from the core. Arms are typically extended away from the body in "airy" postures. The legs perform movements in a position rotated or "turned out" from the hips, requiring flexibility in the muscles of the hips and legs. Balances are often held upon the tips of the toes, known as "en pointe."

The majority of movement is done in upright positions—balanced, locomoting upon, or jumping/leaping and landing upon the feet. This requires both flexibility and strength in the legs and feet. Movement is largely directed away from the floor, as the ballet dancer continually strives to create the illusion of weightlessness and effortlessness. The ultimate visual goal is elevation and elongation of the "lines" of the body, and of movement.

Classical Positions for the Feet and Arms in Ballet

- **First Position**
  - Feet: heels touching, toes turned out
  - Arms: both arms held in front of the torso symmetrically, hands at waist level, fingers reaching toward midline
- **Second Position**
  - Feet: separated laterally at about shoulder width, toes turned out
  - Arms: both arms extended open and held symmetrically out to the sides, hands between the shoulders and ribcage
- **Third Position**
  - Feet: heel of one foot against the instep of the other foot, toes turned out
  - Arms: arm corresponding with front foot overhead as in fifth position, arm corresponding with back foot open to the side as in second position
- **Fourth Position**
  - Feet: separated sagittally, one in front of the other; toes turned out
  - Arms: arm corresponding with front foot in front of the torso as in first position, arm corresponding with back foot overhead as in fifth position

- **Fifth Position**
  - Feet: heel of one foot against the big toe of the other foot, toes turned out
  - Arms: both arms extended overhead, fingers reaching toward midline

Barre Sequence of Warm-Up Exercises

Term	Translation	Description	Desired physical effects
Plié	to bend	bending and straightening the knees while ankles are turned out	warms leg muscles and ankles, prepares the hip flexors for turnout and alignment
Tendu	to extend or stretch	slide foot along floor to a fully pointed line (doesn't leave floor)	warm/articulate foot and ankle; strengthen foot against floor
Dégagé	to disengage	brush through tendu and lift a few inches off the floor	warm foot/ankle/calf; build quickness and turnout control
Rond de Jambe	circle of the leg	trace a smooth circular path on the floor with a pointed foot	warm foot/ankle/calf/thigh; activate hip rotators (turnout)
Developpé	to develop or grow	draw foot up the standing leg, then unfold and extend	warm hips/thighs; build control through hip flexors/quads and turnout
Frappé	to strike	strike/brush foot from cou-de-pied to a pointed extension	build speed/coordination; strengthen feet and lower legs
Battement	to beat	quick brush out and close (jeté/dégagé)	warm legs/feet; build speed and stamina

Center Work

Once the barre warm-up is finished, dancers move to the center of the floor to complete exercises that develop strength, balance, and movement control on both sides of the body. These exercises include:

- **Tendu** → Stretching of the foot along the floor, away from the standing leg
- **Adagio** → Slow, sustained movements that often incorporate developpés and balances such as penchés
- **Turns From Corner** → These include piqué, chaîné, and similar turns that move the dancer across the floor.
- **Turns at Center** → These include pirouette and fouetté turns, in which the dancer remains in one place on the floor.
- **Petit allegro** → Small, quick jumps in place, such as changements, temps levés, and assemblés
- **Grand allegro** → Large jumps or leaps which move the dancer across the floor, such as grandes jetés or tours jetés
- **Reverence** → The slow port-de-bras and "bow" at the end of class to acknowledge gratitude to the teacher

Pas De Deux

The pas de deux (French for "step of two") is a duet in which two ballet dancers perform together as partners. Usually, a male dancer provides support for a female dancer, allowing her to perform more numerous turns, longer balances, and higher leaps than she could on her own.

There are four main movements involved in a pas de deux:

- **Promenades** → The female dancer balances en pointe, and the male rotates her in a circle.
- **Turns** → The female dancer turns repeatedly, and the male stabilizes her from behind.
- **Lifts** → The male dancer lifts the female dancer into the air.
- **Leaps** → The female dancer leaps on her own, and the male dancer helps her leap higher. Or, the female dancer leaps, and the male dancer catches her before she lands.

The pas de deux usually follows a classical form that includes these sections:

- **Entreé** → Dancers first come together
- **Adagio** → Slow, sustained movement together
- **Variations** → Usually one for each dancer to show individual skills
- **Coda** → Reuniting to end the pas de deux

Ballet's Entrance into the United States

In the 1930s, a Russian dancer and choreographer named George Balanchine, who had been with Sergei Diaghilev's company Ballets Russes, was invited by a patron to bring his talents to America. In 1934, Balanchine opened The School of American Ballet in New York. In 1948, he opened the New York City Ballet, which became the premiere ballet company in the United States. Balanchine is considered the founder of the modern classical method of ballet.

Balanchine's style emphasized intense speed and intricacy of steps (requiring great agility and strength), unconventional arm positions, an especially deep plié (requiring great flexibility), and strong lines. Choreographically, there is an emphasis on interplay between choreography and the accompanying musical structure. The choreography is often very dramatic, requiring dancers to be especially expressive.

Modern Dance: Core Vocabulary & Technique

Impetus for the Development of Modern Dance

Modern dance was a response to the strictures of ballet, showing its first glimmers in the early-20th century when Loie Fuller, Isadora Duncan, and Ruth St. Denis all began showcasing their own styles of dance, eliciting great response from a world ready for change, ease, and freedom. Spectators familiar only with vaudeville had never before seen the kind of imaginative, innovative, and evocative movement being performed by these women, and though there was a measure of ridicule and distrust, popular opinion overwhelmingly supported the new developments.

The subsequent generation of dancers—notably Doris Humphrey, Robert Weidman, and Martha Graham, all students of Ruth St. Denis and Ted Shawn—brought modern dance to fruition as an unprecedented art form defined by individual movement philosophies. Each of them refined their personal styles into longstanding teaching methods still being taught today, and spawned multiple generations of modern dancers, teachers, and choreographers.

Practices and Movement Philosophies of Modern Dance

Although modern dance shares some features with ballet, it was largely a response to—and rebellion against—ballet. It took shape under a banner of individual exploration into natural, instinctive, expressive movement styles, and has developed ever since into its own always-evolving entity that encompasses as many styles of movement as there are dancers.

Movement philosophies prevalent in modern dance are: an emphasis on coordinating movement with the breath; a focus on shifting the weight freely across the feet, hands, shoulders, pelvis, spine, or any other body part that touches the floor; the use of an articulated spine and the limbs; a focus on working with the floor and the force of gravity; and an intention to explore or express a personal, intellectual, emotional, design, philosophical, or other concept through movement.

Comparing the Ways Modern Dance and Ballet Use Space

Modern dance shares ballet's movement vocabulary, and the two employ the same physical forces to produce similar motions—bending in plié in order to push off the floor and lift the body into the air, for instance. The movement intention and aesthetic of ballet and modern dance, however, are fundamentally different.

To describe the difference between ballet and modern dance in simple terms, whereas ballet is "up," modern dance is "down." Body posture and movement intention in ballet are focused on elongating and elevating, while the focus in modern dance is on grounding and spreading. This results in dramatically different shapes between the two forms.

Another main difference is that modern dance incorporates the use of floor work. All of the limbs and sometimes even the head come into contact with the floor, challenging notions of verticality and introducing the mover to possibilities of inversion and balances upon unusual body parts. Conversely, ballet largely requires the dancer to remain upright, atop the feet and legs.

Technical Features of Modern Dance

Although part of the heritage of modern dance rests upon the freedom of each dancer to find a personal way of moving, nearly all styles of modern dance share certain features. These include:

- **Parallel Foot Positioning** → Feet are situated in alignment under the hips, and the toes point forward.
- **Flexed Feet** → This is comparable to the pointed toe of ballet. It communicates humanity, capability, locomotion, defiance, homeliness, or comedy, or it can be used to add another angle to the visual design of a dance.
- **Groundedness** → This is an affinity for the floor and the force of gravity that takes a dancer there. It allows for the use of momentum in swings, and for "pushing into" the floor to gain greater height in jumps and extensions.
- **Weight Sharing in Contact Work** → Partners distribute their combined weight in optimal proportions to make shapes and movements while in close contact.

Parallel Foot Positioning

Parallel foot positioning, in which the feet are situated in alignment under the hips with the toes pointing forward, is the most natural foot orientation for human locomotion. This is, in fact, the orientation humans use to walk. We are physiologically designed as predators, with two eyes in the front of our heads and limbs that naturally swing sagittally during locomotion. The feet, as extensions of the legs, also move in a sagittal back-and-forth motion. This motion is aided by the straightforward orientation of the toes and the corresponding capacity to balance weight evenly across the feet.

Modern dance pioneers, in their quest for more natural and instinctual movement, rejected the awkward, outwardly rotated stance required of ballet dancers in favor of the more natural parallel position. Occasionally, this is referred to by ballet dancers as "sixth position," an allusion to parallel position's addition to the five classical (and turned-out) ballet positions.

Floor Work

Because of modern dance's emphasis on groundedness, a connection to the floor, and a working cooperation with gravity—as well as its openness to experimentation—the modern form of dance involves more floor work than other forms of dance, such as ballet or tap. In these forms, dancers usually stand on their feet.

Floor work can be done while kneeling, crouching, on hands and knees, sitting, or lying on the floor. Combinations of these positions can also be used. Movements can include crawling, rolling, scooting, dragging, slithering, etc. Often, movements at this level can express ideas of earth, gravity, weight, debasement, filth, ugliness, evil, disadvantage, poverty, sadness, or dejection, among others.

Floor work also supports the modern ethos by affording opportunities to use unconventional body parts for balance, locomotion, and pivoting (as in shoulder stands, dragging the prone body forward with the elbows, or spinning on one sitz bone), as well as to invert the body in unfamiliar orientations.

Martha Graham, Doris Humphrey and Charles Weidman, and Lester Horton

Martha Graham's technique involves a dramatic "contraction and release," wherein dancers use an explosive exhalation to facilitate a corresponding deep muscular contraction in the torso. Graham technique also emphasizes weight moving into the floor and a spiral image for off-center or off-balance movement.

Doris Humphrey's style explores "fall and recovery," the body's interplay with gravity. It involves the body falling into chaos and then returning to equilibrium. Charles Weidman added his own talent for transforming everyday movement into the absurd or dramatic to the technique. In later years, Jose Limón continued and refined Humphrey's style, ensuring it would continue to be practiced for generations.

Lester Horton's technique appears in the "lateral T" shape his dancers assume—a one-leg balance with the torso tilted off-center and the other leg extended to the side in a counterbalance. Horton's emphasis on strengthening movements and on flat backs, pelvic hinges, and oppositional movement created powerful dancers capable of sustaining constant movement.

Later Modern Dance Techniques That Are Taught and Performed Today

The technique of Merce Cunningham, abstract as it appears to many, has had a far-reaching effect on the modern dance canon. Cunningham created dances without any attached historical, cultural, or philosophical meanings, and subjected the elements of his dances—music, sets, costumes, even movement segments and dancers' spatial relationships—to chance during each individual performance.

Erick Hawkins developed an effortless "free flow" technique that released tension in the body through an emphasis on weight, placement, impulse, immediacy, and movement dynamics. As a result, he freed up the body for greater flexibility and strength, and also freed the mind so it could be more deeply engaged in the movement.

Paul Taylor's technique draws from everyday gestures and movements such as sitting, crawling, rolling, walking, and running to explore and expand upon fundamental human states and their interactions with dynamic athleticism. Taylor's choreography often embodies thematic opposites of dark and light and tragedy and comedy simultaneously.

Improvisation as an Exploratory Offshoot of Modern Dance

Judson Church dancer Steve Paxton originated the practice of contact improvisation in the 1970s, focusing on the physical and energetic points of contact between two or more dancers and the way they could initiate movement through the dancers' responses. These responses could vary in terms of weight, energy, and momentum. The form can be practiced by people with a range of physical abilities or physical limitations, as the form's main emphasis is on sensitivity to the movements and energy of other dancers, as well as on inventive ways of creating movements by using the perceived information.

Begun as a subset of post-modern dance, contact improvisation has become its own distinct form with diverse manifestations. It is used by some as a meditative movement practice, by others as a specialized form of social dance, by others as a means of movement research to generate choreographic material, and by the highly skilled as a form of dance suitable for performances in concert settings.

Traditional Terminology and Form Employed in Modern Dance Classes

Modern dance emphasizes the finding of an individual, personally authentic movement style over the codification of form and structure. Individual styles are often informed by the specific focus of a dancer's creative exploration and the needs of the physical body.

Modern dance has no standardized terminology, so even though it uses many standard terms from its predecessor, ballet (plié, tendu, and battement, for example), these are augmented by countless other movement words that range from basic commands (bend, contract, and swing, for instance) to terms specific to one teacher's movement philosophy.

Modern dance classes do not share a universally codified structure or sequence, although, like ballet classes, they begin with warm-up movements. Instead of being performed at a barre, however, they are usually performed at center, sometimes beginning from a supine position on the floor. From warm-ups, classes then progress through a series of increasingly demanding movements before finishing with the learning and performing of a choreographic combination.

Jazz & Tap: Core Vocabulary & Technique

Practices and Movement Philosophies of Tap Dance

In its simplest characterization, tap dance can be explained as dance that creates its own rhythm. It involves making music on the floor with the feet while wearing shoes with taps on the toes and heels. Tap dance originated in the 1800s. Originally, it was a combination of Irish step dance and English clog dance and satirical versions of African slaves' dances.

Early tap evolved into two distinct styles: the buck-and-wing (fast and dynamic, performed in wooden-soled shoes) and softshoe (a smooth, fluid style done in soft leather-soled shoes). As the form developed, elements of current social dances were incorporated, and stylistic elements of jazz, ballet, ballroom, and modern dance were also introduced.

Today, tap is loosely divided into two styles: rhythm tap, which focuses on musical patterns, and Broadway tap, which emphasizes the form's dance aspects. All styles of tap incorporate the syncopation of beats, as well as the practice of improvisation.

Tap Dancing

Rhythm tap focuses on the musical (acoustic) aspect of tapping, in which dancers express themselves through the rhythms they create. This style tends to be grounded into the floor to focus on the feet. Rhythm tap dancers are called "hoofers," and consider themselves part of the jazz musical tradition. The origins of both forms can be traced back to nightclubs, when rhythm tappers would set the tempo for jazz bands. Famous "hoofers" include Bill "Bojangles" Robinson, Sammy Davis Jr., Gregory Hines, and Savion Glover.

Broadway, or show, tap focuses on the design and dance (aesthetic) aspect of tapping, and incorporates elements of modern, ballet, jazz, and social dances. Hallmarks of this style include the use of choreographed movements of the arms and torso as well as the legs and feet, and a lighter, more lyrical style than rhythm tap. Noted Broadway tappers include Fred Astaire, Gene Kelly, and Ann Miller.

Building-Block Steps in Tap Dance

- **Tap** → striking the floor with an immediate release; can be done with the heel or the ball of the foot
- **Step** → placing the ball of the foot on the floor with a weight change
- **Touch** → placing the ball of the foot on the floor without a weight change
- **Stamp** → placing the entire foot on the floor with a weight change
- **Stomp** → placing the entire foot on the floor without a weight change
- **Toe** → striking the floor with the tip of the foot, with or without a weight change
- **Brush/Scuff** → lightly striking the floor in an outward sweeping motion (brush with ball, scuff with heel)
- **Shuffle** → forward brush followed by a backward brush
- **Flap** → forward brush followed by a step
- **Slap** → forward brush followed by a touch
- **Ball Change** → two steps in sequence, one on each foot; the first step gets less weight than the second
- **Hop** → leaving the ground and landing on the same foot
- **Jump** → leaving the ground and landing on the other foot

Time Steps

Time steps in tap dance are recognizable rhythmic combinations of steps, and are considered basics that should be mastered by all tappers. They are commonly categorized as singles, doubles, and triples, depending on the number of movements (and corresponding sounds) on the second and sixth counts of an eight-count phrase.

A basic single time step is structured similar to this:

- Right shuffle/left hop/right step/left flap/right step; repeat on other side; then break, which consists of right shuffle/left hop/right step/left flap/right flap/left flap/right step. The classical pattern of a time step is two bars repeated three times, a two-bar break, and the two bars repeated three times again.
- Many times, tap dancers will begin with a preparatory hop or step on the "eight," or the "and-eight," count of an eight-count phrase. The first step of a time step is also often varied. It may be a step, a shuffle, or a hop.

Origins of Jazz Dance

Jazz dance began to emerge in America in the 1940s, beginning as an offshoot of tap dancing and sharing its close attention to the syncopated musical rhythms of jazz music. By the 1950s, it had left behind tap's necessity of creating audible rhythms, and had evolved into its own distinct form by incorporating elements of ballet, theatrical dance, social dances, and ethnic traditional dances from many countries. In this way, jazz dance, like America itself, became a "melting pot."

As the influences on jazz broadened, so did its movement style. Increasing numbers of dancers from various backgrounds were attracted to the form, diluting its mainly African American origins and further expanding the form's vocabulary and expressive capabilities. The post-World War II boom created a nervous energy in the country that was perfectly portrayed by the isolations, syncopation, and attitude of jazz.

Practices and Movement Philosophies of Jazz Dance

Like tap from which it evolved, jazz maintained a strong interplay with the accompanying music, but shifted emphasis upward from the feet to the hips, spine, limbs, and head. This created a more sensuous and expressive response to the often syncopated rhythms. Elements of ballet, theatrical, social, and ethnic dance injected a sense of physical prowess into this expression of the cultural climate.

Like modern dance, jazz does not emanate from a system of codified steps. It is more a style of "physical slang," conveying attitude and nonchalance. Over the years, a canon of movements contributed by its practitioners has developed. Improvisation and embellishment are hallmarks of the form, as are movements done in syncopation.

Physically, jazz is embodied in a looseness and fluidity of movement punctuated by sharp rhythmic features and dramatic shapes created by the use of isolations, which involves moving body parts independently of—and often deliberately against—the whole.

Body Isolations in Jazz Dance

Isolations are an identifying feature of jazz dance. They are practiced diligently in technique classes, and are intrinsic to jazz choreography. They are achieved by moving one body part independently of all the others—for example, rolling the head atop a still body—rather than cooperatively moving all body parts in the same manner or direction. Several different isolations are usually employed at once—pulsing a hip to the right while rotating the left hand at the wrist and tossing the head, for instance.

Multiple isolations create the impression that many disparate things are happening at once (which is often the case with the rhythms that accompany the movement, as well as the cultural climate which surrounds jazz dance). As such, isolations are one of the elements that imbue jazz with its characteristic casual virtuosity, its controlled chaos, its ready-for-anything sense of surprise, and its insouciant attitude.

Characteristic Movements of Jazz Dance

- **Jazz Walk** → This is a walk exaggerating the articulations of the limbs and showcasing the attitude and individual style of the dancer.
- **Jazz Square** → This is a step that follows a square pattern on the floor. While facing forward, the dancer steps open right, crosses front left, steps back right, and finishes by stepping open left. The step can be started with either foot.
- **Contraction** → This is a muscular movement in which the abdominal muscles draw back into the body, rounding the back and drawing the pelvis under and forward.
- **Layout** → This is a dramatic extension that requires a dancer to balance on one leg, extend the other leg forward, and "lay back" with the torso, following the line of the extended leg.
- **Hip Isolation** → This involves shifting the hips from side to side while holding the rest of the body motionless.
- **Rib Isolation** → This involves shifting the ribcage from side to side while holding the rest of the body motionless.

Stylistic Points That Distinguish Jazz from Other Performance Dance Forms

- **Jazz Hands** → This is the most recognizable (and easily parodied) feature of jazz, and is a widespread hand posture where the fingers are extended strongly outward from the palm.
- **Snap** → This is the dynamic "hitting" of a position, characterized by an accelerated approach into and an emphatic arrival at a shape, which can then be held for further emphasis. Sometimes, the snap happens during the withdrawal from a shape instead.
- **Head Whip** → This is a kind of snap. The head is tossed or turned from a frontward orientation to the side. It can be extended as an isolation into a full 360-degree head roll.
- **Angular Oppositions** → This involves placing the limbs into positions so that the resulting combination of angles (most visibly created by elbows and knees) is unusual, unnatural, and attention-grabbing.
- **Pelvic Thrusts** → In this jazz move, usually done from a contraction, the pelvis is pressed forcefully forward, often rhythmically, and sometimes with the intention of creating a provocative movement.

Modern Performance Forms of Jazz Dance

Eugene Louis Facciuto, known as Luigi, developed his jazz style as a therapeutic method after a crippling car accident. It is often used by dancers looking for physiological symmetry and integrity. The style emphasizes fluidity, unbroken motion, balance, and smooth transitions. Isolations are done gently.

Gus Giordano, who instituted the Jazz Dance World Congress with the intention of legitimizing jazz dance as a concert form, established an exploratory style. It combines the lifted, elongated upper body and deep pliés of ballet with an earthy, grounded sensibility that moves the entire body and also isolates movement in different parts.

Matt Mattox's physically demanding style emphasizes agility in all areas—rhythmic complexity, simultaneous isolations of arms/feet/head/rib cage, weight transfer, and response/resistance to gravity. Opening barre exercises provide a total warm-up by focusing on each anatomical area.

World & Social Dance: Forms, Vocabulary & Practice

Social Dances That Are Common to All Cultures

Social dance is, by definition, communal dance. It is created for the purpose of affirming a community's shared knowledge, culture, and experiences. The dance steps, as well as the music, costumes, and other accompanying traditions, are handed down from one generation to the next through observation and participation, rather than via a rigid scholastic format.

To best facilitate this informal learning, traditional dance steps are usually simple and somewhat natural. In many cases, steps are based on movements used in the work and daily lives of the people and their ancestors, and so are already familiar to the people learning them. Possible examples of familiar movements are fishermen pulling nets and farmers planting seeds.

Often, steps are rhythmic and feature set foot patterns, as rhythm and patterns are both easy devices for categorizing and recalling information. Most importantly, dances are taught in a fun, social environment, which motivates dancers to learn the dance steps, remember them, and look forward to performing them.

Energy and Intention in Global Folk, Social Dances, and Ballet

Although there are innumerable forms of folk and social dance, all kinds of folk dance share certain characteristics. They are informally and socially communicated by lay people (non-professionals), are shared in a communal place as opposed to a stage, and are taught using a traditional approach. Knowledge of these dances is passed from one generation to the next. The energy in folk dance is communal; it is focused on the entire dancing group as well as on spectators. The atmosphere is relaxed, and the setting is a social and recreational one.

Ballet shares only one characteristic with folk dance: it is taught using a traditional approach. However, knowledge is passed on from teacher to dancer through a rigid training structure. Ballet differs from folk dance in its emphasis on virtuosity and its intention to divide performers from spectators for the performance configuration. The energy in ballet is deeply focused on performance, and on creating an illusion to be enjoyed by spectators. Unlike folk dance, the energy in ballet is not communal.

African Dance Styles

African dances are as varied as the countries that make up the continent itself, but they all share a powerful, integral sense of rhythm and represent a connection with the earth (the land, water, wind, sun, moon, stars, plants, and animals), living people, and the ancestors or deities who watch over humans as they go about their daily lives.

African dances are expressive and often exuberant, even acrobatic. Most are usually done in plié. Foot-stamping using the heel, the ball of the foot, or the entire sole is a common feature. Foot patterns are prominent, and range from simple to extremely complex. The spine is mostly erect, with much articulation as well as freedom of movement in the pelvis. There is great variation in gesture, extension, and/or swinging of the limbs. Frequently, movements are done in repeating patterns. The cue to change movements is often provided by accompanying drummers. Dances can be accompanied by a cappella singing, drums, or other instruments.

Drumming in African Dance

In African music and dance, the sound of the drum is likened to the human heartbeat, as well as the heartbeat of the world—it is considered vitally important. Most African music prominently features at least one, and usually several, types of drums.

Since different drums produce different sounds, they have varying patterns and purposes. The combination of several drum sounds and patterns produces polyrhythms, the "different voices" that give African music its complexity, urgency, and depth.

Drums in African dance do more than keep time for the dancers. In addition to unifying dancers, drummers, and spectators (who regularly become participants), they also control the movements of dancers in many ways. Different drum sounds and rhythms call for different movements, allowing for complexity in grouping and timing in choreography. "Drum breaks," recognizable changes in drumming patterns, are signals to change movement patterns.

Indian Dance Styles

Dance styles in India can be divided into two groups: folk styles, which reflect the everyday life and culture of villagers and rural peoples; and classical styles, which require extensive training in order to perform. Indian dances often tell stories of people, animals, or deities, and all dances are closely associated with the geographical area from which they originate.

Folk dances in India are often dedicated to deities—either in supplication for favors, or for celebration and thanks—and are frequently performed by children. Formations include single or double circles, parallel rows, and sometimes even pyramids, which are often divided by sex. Often, participants play instruments while simultaneously dancing.

Indian classical dance requires rigorous balance, control of the torso and center of gravity, and well-developed coordination to balance rhythmic footwork and precise foot patterns with multiple gestural movements of the hands, feet, and eyes to communicate a variety of mental states and emotions.

Hula

Hula is a complex dance form encompassing many dances native to Hawaii. It employs a vast vocabulary of fluid hand motions representing words, concepts, or natural elements. The dance is accompanied by traditional instruments and chants. Both women and men can perform various hula dances while seated or standing (or sometimes both). Hula is usually performed with bare feet.

Hawaiian culture is passed down through memorized chants relating legends about creation, the natural world, deities, royalty, and ancestors. Hula dance, performed simultaneously, illustrates these stories with a variety of movements that range from established foot patterns and knee and hip undulations to acrobatic combat and juggling sequences.

Great emphasis is placed on authenticity of interpretation, precision of the movement vocabulary, and correct presentation of the prescribed elements of costuming for each dance. Every fold of fabric, leaf, flower, and ripple of the hand adds meaning to the story that hula tells.

Flamenco

Handed down from the form's Romany, or Gypsy, progenitors, flamenco is a dramatic dance form that features intricate percussive footwork, stylized arm and hand movements, and a proud, regal carriage of the torso and head to communicate themes of passion, pride, and defiance.

Flamenco can be danced solo or with a partner. When performed by partners, there is often fierce eye contact and challenging attitudes, but very little physical contact. Traditionally, dancers are accompanied by a corps of musicians and powerful singers, though they are capable of accompanying themselves with complicated rhythmic foot patterns and/or castanets, which are wooden handheld percussion instruments.

Traditional costumes for men are stylized versions of male toreador costumes, which include tight black pants and cropped jackets. Women wear form-fitting dresses with heavily ruffled skirts that are sometimes tossed or "switched" for added dramatic effect. Both sexes wear hard-soled boots to amplify the rhythmic patterns created by the feet.

European Dance Styles

Greek dances feature rhythmic dragging, hopping, or leaping. Dancers hold their hands raised or at the shoulders. Often, a dancer at one end of a line or circle formation performs acrobatic jumps and kicks. Dancers move in the main direction for a certain number of steps. They then move a few steps back in the opposite direction to end the phrase.

Balkan dances have a similar formation as Greek dances—dancers perform rhythmic hops and steps while holding on to each others' shoulders. However, they are performed to Balkan regional music, which features quick, repeating, hypnotic beats and a nonspecific meter.

Dances of England, Ireland, and Scotland feature rhythmic stepping and hopping patterns. These dances are performed in single lines, double lines, or circles. Individuals or couples face and move around each other. In Morris dances and other group dances, individuals face each other. Props such as sticks, hoops, flexible swords, garlands, or handkerchiefs may be used.

Native North American Dance Styles

Native American dances can represent the material world, depicting daily activities such as tracking or hunting, or the motion of the grass or water. They can also represent the spirit world. The hoop dance, for instance, represents the circle of life.

The subjects of dances can also illustrate the differences among nomadic tribes, hunting tribes, and stationary agricultural tribes. Dances by hunters honor respected animals upon which they depend, and dances by farmers depict the seasons, plants, and the movements used to sow and harvest crops.

Many Native American dances incorporate rhythmic stepping and stamping, which is done mostly while dancers are standing upright or bent slightly forward at the waist. The weight is on the balls of the feet and the bent knees. The dancers often move in circles. A single dancer may spin around individually, or a group may trace a path around a central point. Elaborate costumes are also integral to this form.

South American and Central American Dance Styles

Partner dances done by couples to a variety of accompanying Latin rhythms are one type of social dance popular across Central America and South America. Popular dance forms in these regions include samba, rumba, mambo, cha-cha, conga, cumbia, salsa, merengue, and tango. These dances incorporate basic rhythmic patterns of forward-and-back, side-to-side, or combination steps, which are embellished by rolling the hips and shoulders, varying body positions, and adding accents and turns.

Many indigenous and Spanish-speaking South American cultures were influenced by the importation of slaves from Africa, and this influence appears not only in many of the rhythms and movements used in the popular social dances, but also in various folk dance forms done by groups of men and women, which contain a wide variety of movements depicting love, slavery, many forms of labor, and even war. Examples of the latter are the acrobatic dance-combat forms of el juego de maní and capoeira.

Baile Folklórico

Baile folklórico is a performance style of dance combining the footwork, costuming, and musical accompaniment of Latin folk dances with the exacting choreography and exaggerated positions of ballet.

Costumes are important in this style of dance. Their design is influenced by regional identities and aesthetics. In general, men wear (sometimes ornately embroidered) pants, short jackets, and wide-brimmed hats. Women wear ribbons in their hair, ruffled blouses, voluminous, heavily ruffled skirts, and (occasionally) shawls. The latter two pieces can be used to further dramatize the female dancer's swirling, sweeping arm movements. Often, both sexes wear hard-soled boots, which emphasize foot rhythms.

Technically partner dances, baile folklórico dances are often performed by groups of couples that form circles or rows on the floor. Often, choreography involves the partners facing each other. The men maintain a closed frame with their arms, while the women sweep the edges of their skirts into swirling arcs that can travel above their heads.

African American Social Dances That Contributed to Later Jazz Technique

- **Cakewalk** → This was a dance performed by couples. Dancers joined hands and walked in straight lines to form a box, often in an exaggeratedly solemn fashion (the dance could involve the use of high kicks, leaned-back torsos, waving canes, etc.). It parodied white ballroom dance styles.
- **Black Bottom** → This was a "challenge" dance that purportedly originated in the mimicry of a cow's hind legs stuck in the mud. It was characterized by side-to-side steps, hops forward and back (while slapping the buttocks), and hip gyrations.
- **Charleston** → This featured jaunty forward-and-back steps with a kick. It could be performed by individuals or partners. It sometimes incorporated rotating the knees inward and outward and crossing the hands back and forth over them.
- **Jitterbug** → This was a partner dance in the swing style. A distinctive rhythm was created by the side-step-side-step-cross-back pattern.
- **Lindy Hop** → This was a partner swing dance with a signature slow-quick-quick (or sometimes quick-quick-slow) rhythm. It provided opportunities for numerous dynamic and acrobatic embellishments, such as swings, kicks, lifts, and throws.

Movements of European and Early North American Social Dances

Traditional dances from England, Scotland, Ireland, and Wales share many characteristics. These dances influenced the social dances of the early United States, resulting in the popular American dance style known as square dancing. Feet movements mostly consist of a rhythmic, bouncing locomotion step, which propels individuals and couples through the floor patterns. The arms are relaxed, and arm movement is largely restricted to what is necessary for dancing with a partner.

Floor patterns can be roughly divided into lines and circles (or the adapted squares). Line dances, which include reels, usually consist of two lines, with the dancers facing each other. Often, dancers venture from their places in line to the center, where they engage with a partner or another dancer before returning to their place in line. Circle dances, such as schottisches, provide couples and individuals with the opportunity to interweave their stepping patterns and "greet" other dancers as they make their way around a room.

Teaching Techniques from a Variety of Genres, Cultures, and Time Periods

In some cases, teachers can make use of community resources to broaden students' dance horizons. If the surrounding community is home to any professional performers, teachers, companies, or recreational groups that specialize in a particular kind of dance, their input can be especially inspiring to students.

A visit from a guest teacher or a performer with specialized knowledge can offer not only visual stimulation in the form of accompanying costumes and electrifying demonstrations, but likely also a deeper familiarity with entertaining lore, as well as techniques and creative teaching methods intrinsic to the form.

Alternatively, a field trip to see a performance by a soloist or a group can be equally exciting, providing the opportunity to witness firsthand how the dances look, sound, and feel in their natural forms. If attending a live performance is not possible, video footage of particular dance forms is a useful option, especially in the study of historical dances.

In order to acquaint students with the immense breadth of the dance world, it is necessary to present them with opportunities to both see and learn to perform dances from a variety of genres, cultures, and time periods.

In many public schools, dance classes are broken into sections, and focus on a different kind of dance each week or every couple of weeks. For example, one section might focus on the concert forms of jazz, tap, ballet, modern, and hip hop. Another might focus on folk dances from Greece, India, Western Africa, the British Isles, and North America. Then, there might be another section that focuses on Italian Renaissance court dances, early American square dances, and social dances of the 1950s and 1960s.

Each dance form should be introduced and accompanied by a discussion of its geographical and historical origins, accompanying customs, cultural purposes, costumes and other identifying factors, influences, and similarities to other forms.

Dancer Health, Safety & Injury Prevention

Healthy Lifestyle

Basic practices of a healthy lifestyle include: eating healthy foods in reasonable amounts at proper intervals to maintain blood sugar levels, drinking enough water to keep the body adequately hydrated at all times, getting sufficient rest to allow regeneration of muscular tissue and restore neurological function, achieving and maintaining sufficient lung capacity to deliver adequate oxygen to the brain, maintaining a safe weight that is neither too far over nor too far below an individual's ideal weight, maintaining a clear and strong mental focus when working, and relaxing both physically and mentally when not working.

These basics can be augmented by acquiring skills more specific to the demands of dancing, including: understanding one's own body type and its limitations, capacities, and needs; having a clear idea of one's individual joint alignment and any specific joints that require rehabilitation or modification; and becoming familiar with one's own specific conditioning needs (to achieve increased strength, flexibility, coordination, endurance, etc.).

Proper Blood Sugar Levels and Nutrition

All dancers must take care not to eat too much or too little. However, other equally important concerns related to eating include timing, availability, and nutrients.

Eating healthy food at frequent enough intervals to maintain blood sugar levels is a must. However, most dancers face a constant lack of money and time, and sometimes must resort to fast food or whatever is available, whenever they can get it. Additionally, traditional eating patterns (such as three large meals a day, as is common in America) don't fit the lifestyle and needs of dancers.

To address this issue, many dancers carry nuts, dried fruits, yogurt, prepared energy bars, apples, citrus fruits, granola, or other affordable, portable foods. This allows them to eat small amounts of healthy foods several times a day. This helps to avoid the "spike and crash" blood sugar pattern that traditional eating patterns can induce.

Nutrients

Dancers need fluids more consistently and in greater amounts than non-dancers. They sweat out high volumes of fluid every day, which must be replaced constantly. Dehydration can result in muscle cramps, weakness, dizziness, and fainting.

Half or more of a dancer's diet should consist of carbohydrates, which provide muscles with energy. Complex carbohydrates (cereal, pasta, rice, grains, etc.) are preferred over simple sugars, which can cause blood sugar to rise and fall quickly.

About 15 percent of a dancer's diet should consist of protein, which maintains tissue integrity in muscles, tendons, ligaments, and bones. Complete proteins are commonly found in meat, poultry, and fish, and in combinations of soy, vegetables, grains, and nuts.

At least 20 percent of a dancer's diet should consist of fat, which provides energy, helps with vitamin absorption, and improves resistance to disease. Avocadoes, nuts, and seafood are rich in fats, but low in saturated ("bad") fats.

Vitamins and minerals are also important, as they help the body carry out its functions.

Weight

Physically, excess weight places extra stress on a dancer's joints, muscles, and circulatory and respiratory systems. It can exacerbate traumatic injuries and accelerate the effects of chronic or cumulative injuries. In performance, the height of jumps can be lower, choreographic shapes can appear less clear if limbs are obstructed by extra tissue, and lifts can be more difficult.

However, a more prevalent problem within the dance world is that dancers are often underweight. This is often a result of the field's prevailing and extreme emphasis on thinness. This is especially true for ballet dancers, who are at a disproportionately higher risk for eating disorders such as anorexia nervosa and bulimia. Extremely low levels of body fat also place dancers at a greater risk of exhaustion and disease. Young dancers who are underweight can experience a delay in the onset of menstruation. The resulting lack of estrogen can impede bone development, leading to advanced osteoporosis at unnaturally young ages.

TIME MANAGEMENT

Dance is not always valued in society—and even less often compensated—so many dancers must fit their dancing in between school, day jobs, family, and other demands. Even professional dancers must keep rigorous training, rehearsal, and touring schedules. Finding time and opportunities for proper nutrition, rest, and relaxation (physical and mental) is often difficult.

Long work or school days can mean late rehearsals, which cuts into the dancer's sleep and results in fatigue. This puts dancers at risk for injury. Tight daytime schedules or limited budgets often make grocery shopping difficult, so dancers must often eat what they can, when they can. Frequently, the foods that are easiest to access are sugary, salty, or caffeinated foods from vending machines and convenience stores. These conditions, in addition to the daily demands of classes and rehearsals, combine to create heightened levels of neuromuscular tension and mental stress for dancers.

CONDITIONING

Many dancers believe that going to dance class every day is enough to adequately condition their bodies. However, this is not generally true. In order to meet the physical demands of classes, rehearsals, and performances, nearly all dancers need a separate conditioning program based upon their body type and individual strengths, weaknesses, alignment issues, movement behavior patterns, and needs for strength, flexibility, and endurance.

The purpose of dance is to explore the possibilities of human movement and express ideas, thoughts, and meaning—not to transform the body into its best possible shape. In fact, many styles of movement in dance require movements that are quite detrimental to the body's physical integrity. Relying solely upon the daily repetition of those movements for conditioning is a way to damage the body, not strengthen it. A few choreographic styles focus upon enhancing physical integrity, but all dancers should engage in a separate conditioning regimen for optimal performance.

Dancers must cultivate a broad and comprehensive range of physical attributes to support dynamic daily movement at a consistently high level. These attributes include:

- Strength in skeletal, muscular, and connective tissues (tendons and ligaments) to provide stability, balance, and the capacity to move limbs easily against gravity and resistance
- Flexibility and muscular elasticity in order to achieve full range of motion and complete extensions are important attributes. While joint mobility and flexibility are the dancer's holy grail, one should always aim to balance these attributes with stability to prevent injuries.
- Muscular endurance, in order to sustain movement (especially repetitive movements during classes or rehearsals) over time without fatigue or injury
- Cardiopulmonary endurance, so the body will be able to continue delivering blood and oxygen to all parts of the body during sustained aerobic exercise
- Neuromuscular coordination, for the precise performance of complex movements as well as the ability to respond kinesthetically to cues of structural misalignment

Muscular strength is the muscles' ability to exert tension against resistance. It allows a dancer to hold the integrity of positions against the weight of gravity or his or her own (or another dancer's) limbs and body, and allows a dancer to stop a moving object or person by overcoming its momentum.

Exercises that require the dancer to overcome gravity to suspend and move weight (holding a plank or completing push-ups, leg lifts, presses, curls, pull-ups, and even pliés and rélevés, for example) or press against resistance (using ab/adduction presses or doing sit-ups or crunches) will build strength in the active muscles.

Strengthening exercises involve few repetitions and great resistance or weight. Because dancers move through a myriad of positions instead of holding particular ones, it is recommended that strength exercises be performed through the entire range of motion, rather than "contracting in place." Slow movement is preferred over fast, as it allows the dancer to focus on and address weak spots within his or her range of motion.

Endurance is the ability to continue activity over time. Muscular endurance is a muscle's ability to contract over time; cardiorespiratory endurance is the ability to maintain aerobic activity over time.

Muscular endurance exercises involve light resistance or weight and many repetitions, as in ballet barre exercises such as dégagés and frappes, or any repeating muscle contracting exercises. It takes mental discipline to continue working consciously through the boredom that repetition induces. The familiar "burning" sensation in a muscle signals that muscular endurance is reaching its limit; generally, performing five repetitions past that point will increase endurance.

Cardiovascular endurance is developed by continuous activity to exercise the tissues of the heart and lungs and force them to carry out their respective functions. Activities can include walking, running, bicycling, swimming, or any activity that elevates the heart rate. To increase cardiovascular endurance, 15 minutes of daily activity at the "target" heart rate is required. To achieve this, it is necessary to complete 20 to 30 minutes of aerobic activity every day.

Warm-Ups

Warming up before dancing prepares the body to handle the impending demands of a class or performance by gradually accelerating the heart rate, stretching and raising the temperature in the muscles, lubricating tissues surrounding joints, and focusing the mind on the task at hand. Warm-ups almost always involve muscle stretches and joint articulations, and can include repetitive movements, strategic muscle contractions, and aerobic activities such as jogging or jumping.

Cooling down after dancing is possibly even more important than warming up, as it prevents blood from pooling in tissues and causing soreness in muscles. Because many dance classes end with the highest-energy, highest-intensity movements, cool-downs should involve slowly decreasing the intensity of movement and slowing down the heart. This can be done by walking, rolling, or performing other easeful movements, as well as by stretching the muscles to reduce tension.

Flexibility

Muscle flexibility allows for mobility and an enhanced range of motion in the joints. High kicks, deep curls, and fluid spinal undulation all owe their pleasing shapes to muscle flexibility. Flexibility exercises should elongate muscles only; joint-stabilizing ligaments should never be stretched.

When stretching, one must overcome the body's natural stretch reflex: the automatic contraction of a muscle immediately after it has been stretched. This can be achieved by sustaining a stretch for a long time, using a gentle pulsing (NOT bouncing) stretch, or reciprocal inhibition, where the opposing muscle group is forcefully contracted during a stretch. Conscious use of the breath during stretches can enhance their effect.

It should be emphasized that too much flexibility creates joint misalignment, resulting in injuries. A suitable level of strength and stability must accompany mobility in order to maintain the structural integrity of the body. Dancers should take this into consideration when developing and implementing a conditioning program.

Footwear

Modern dancers do not typically wear shoes in class or during performances. Some may wear ballet or jazz shoes or toeless socks (often worn by lyrical dancers) upon the ball of the foot.

Ballet slippers are made of soft leather with a suede sole, and are secured with an elastic strap across the top. Pointe shoes are essentially a satin-wrapped cardboard box that fits around the toes, with padding stuffed inside to give support when en pointe.

Jazz shoes usually cover almost the entire foot, are made of the same soft leather as ballet shoes, and can have a split sole that is also made of suede. Some have a slight heel. Jazz sneakers are more like split-soled athletic shoes, providing added support and stability.

Tap shoes are more rigid to protect against impact. They come in flat and heeled varieties, and have metal taps on the heels and toes.

Appropriate Clothing

In all dance classes, clothes must allow ease of movement, whether they are fitted or loose. There should be no extraneous pieces that might catch, such as zippers, buttons, or snaps. No jewelry should be worn. Layering clothing is a common strategy used by dancers. They wear many layers at the beginning of the class, and then shed them as the body warms up.

In ballet classes, form-fitting leotards and tights are the norm, giving the teacher a clear vision of the lines of each student's form. Leg warmers, arm warmers, nylon dance pants, and small wraparound sweaters or shrugs are commonly worn as top layers.

Modern dance favors looser, comfortable rehearsal clothes that are easy to move in. Dancers may wear leotards and tights, as well as sweat pants, tank tops, and shorts. Sweatshirts and t-shirts are commonly worn when clothing is layered. Jazz and tap dancers often mix up the dress codes of modern dance and ballet based on their individual preferences.

Studio Conditions

Studio flooring for dance classes should be slightly flexible to protect dancers' joints. "Sprung" floors are ideal, though expensive, but even traditional wood is better than concrete or hard tile. Carpet should never be used, as it impedes movement and can cause burns. Floors should be swept before each class, and should be free of protrusions (nails, fixtures, etc.).

Room temperature is also important, as dancers must be warm enough to prevent muscle tightness, but not so warm as to overheat once activity becomes intense. If a room is cold and the teacher cannot change the temperature, layering clothing and completing extensive warm-up exercises may help.

Room size and capacity are also important factors. Nothing in a studio is more dangerous than a moving dancer, especially in a crowded class. Courtesy, vigilance, and care should be used at all times to avoid colliding with other dancers, striking another dancer with a limb, or being struck by the limb of a fellow dancer.

Dance Floor Surface

Though different kinds of dance require different types of floors, in general, the flooring must be able to "give" slightly under a dancer's weight, especially when the dancer lands after performing jumps and leaps.

The unyielding hardness of concrete and hard tile floors transfers the shock of impact entirely into the bones, causing stress and injuries. Possible injuries include shin splints, cartilage deterioration, plantar fasciitis, compression, and hairline fractures.

"Sprung" floors are optimal. In these, several padded or flexible layers are covered with a wooden top surface. The second best types of floors are traditional wooden floors. "Sprung" and wooden floors may be covered with marley vinyl, a non-slip surface that provides traction, but still allows turns. Carpet should never be used, as it impedes movement and can cause burns.

The hard-soled shoes worn to perform dances such as tap, Irish step, and flamenco can make small dents and divots in wooden floors. If at all possible, these wooden floors should be used solely for dance classes during which hard-soled shoes are worn, and no others.

Performance Venue Conditions

One cannot assume performance flooring will be better than studio flooring. For ballet, modern, and jazz performances, the stage will ideally have a "sprung" or wooden floor covered with marley. For performances of tap and other dance styles that involve the use of hard-soled shoes, marley is not necessary, but a wooden stage surface is helpful.

The temperature in many theaters is notoriously hard to control, and in nontraditional venues there may be no control at all. Dancers should bring enough clothes to heavily layer them in case the temperature is extremely cold and plenty of water in case the temperature is extremely hot.

Lighting can affect even experienced dancers. Bright footlights or sidelights can blot out established landmarks in a dancer's field of vision, causing disorientation and even dizziness. Completing a number of rehearsals with full lighting is recommended.

It is also important to inspect backstage areas and the path to the performance area for hazards. Low backstage lighting makes obstacles, overhangs, and black-painted stage equipment difficult to see.

Environmental Factors

A dancer's spatial awareness is affected by the amount of floor space that is available onstage and in the wings. Dancers naturally respond to changing conditions by "pulling in" to conserve movement in a small space, or by expanding out into a larger space. Navigating transition spaces—such as paths from the dressing room to the stage or the "crossover" space behind the stage—requires caution and presence of mind. Avoiding set pieces or other obstacles in a dark space can distract or slow down a dancer.

Lighting is extreme in theaters. Onstage, footlights can be blindingly bright, and sidelights can be set directly at eye level. Backstage areas, by contrast, can be entirely dark. Quick crossovers between the two areas can be especially disorienting.

Venue temperature is also a factor. Dancers require enough heat to keep muscles warm and elastic without overheating, and theater spaces are notoriously hard to heat and/or cool.

Safety Precautions

Theaters, with their moving parts and hidden obstacles, are hazardous places. Production personnel, including performers, must be aware of all possible conditions and hazards.

Dancers should limit the length and volume of conversations, both in person and on cell phones. Texting should be kept to an absolute minimum, and should be done only in the dressing room or outside during breaks—never in the wings or onstage.

Dancers should only go where a stage manager or choreographer directs them, and should promptly follow all instructions.

Performers should not advise or consult with crew members during rehearsals, and should not converse with them at all while a performance is in progress. Distracting a crew member (or a performer) can result in more than missed cues—it could cause a potentially hazardous and possibly dangerous accident.

If a dancer discovers a hazard or needs a question or issue addressed, he or she should immediately report it directly to the stage manager.

Dancers should arrive at the performance venue well-rested, hydrated, reasonably fed, as tension-free as possible, and focused on the production process. This may involve as much coming and going, sitting and waiting, and hurrying and stopping as it does dancing.

Dancers should examine the backstage area and performance space upon arrival. Ideally, the stage manager or a member of the stage crew will familiarize dancers with the pathways between the backstage area and the stage, and will point out any hazards dancers should watch out for.

The stage manager is the person in charge of ensuring the safety of all performers and crew, so he or she will know the location of the venue's first aid kit. It is wise for dancers to be aware of its location as well. As always, dancers should bring enough food, water, extra clothing, and personal supplies to stay comfortable for an extended period of time in the performance venue.

Responsibilities of a Dancer on the Day of a Dance Production

To ensure optimal performance on "show day," a dancer should do the following:

- Before a performance, dancers should get adequate sleep, eat a reasonable amount, drink plenty of water, and do whatever they can to release as much tension as possible from the body. A gentle yoga or Feldenkrais class can help. If a dancer fails to do even one of these, it could result in an impaired performance or even injury.
- As a matter of professionalism and courtesy, dancers should arrive at the performance venue clean and groomed.
- Dancers should arrive promptly at their call time to ensure they will have adequate time for costuming, hair, makeup, warming up, and any last-minute rehearsing, as well as the unforeseen time-wasters that always come up before a show.
- Dancers should also come prepared with enough food, water, extra clothing, and personal supplies to stay comfortable in an uncomfortable environment for several hours.

Traumatic and Chronic Dance Injuries

Traumatic injuries include fractures (possible types of breaks are simple, compound, green stick, spiral, or stress); dislocation or subluxation (a bone removed from its proper place within a joint); sprains (can result when joints are pushed beyond their normal range of motion); strains (muscle tears); concussions (brain injury from a blow to the head, which can result in headache, nausea, dizziness, disorientation, sleepiness, and uneven pupil size); bruises; and cuts, lacerations, or punctures.

Chronic injuries can develop over time due to joint misalignment or muscular imbalance, resulting in painful inflammation and nerve pressure at points of extreme stress. These types of injuries are denoted using the suffix "-itis," and include tendonitis (inflammation of tendons around joints), bursitis (inflammation of fluid sacs in major joints), myositis (inflammation of muscle tissue), and fasciitis (inflammation of the fascia, or sheath of connective fibers that support soft tissues in the body).

R.I.C.E.

R.I.C.E. stands for Rest, Ice, Compression, and Elevation. This approach can be used to treat joint sprains, muscle strains, and some bone injuries. Fractures, however, require immediate professional medical attention.

- **Rest** → The injured individual should cease using the affected body part for at least 48 hours after the injury to ensure it is not repeated. After that, controlling inflammation is paramount, as it will allow the affected tissues to begin healing, and will limit the amount of scar tissue the body will produce.
- **Ice** → Inhibit swelling by applying ice to the injured area for 20 minutes at a time, 4 to 8 times a day. Do not allow the ice to come into direct contact with the skin.
- **Compression** → Inhibit swelling by applying an elastic bandage, brace, air cast, or boot to compress the tissues of the affected area.
- **Elevation** → Inhibit swelling by raising the affected area above the level of the heart.

Repetitive Motion, Overuse, and Chronic/Cumulative Injuries in Dance

Dancers push their bodies every day in order to excel at their work. That frequency of use can turn a condition that might be a small problem for a non-dancer (differing leg lengths, habitual joint misalignment, muscular imbalance, etc.) into a large, potentially career-ending one for a dancer. Even if a dancer begins with a perfectly intact body, many of the regimens necessary to the technique of dance can cause chronic injuries over time. Examples include forcing turnout for ballet and releasing pelvic ligaments for jazz.

Additionally, in order to constantly explore how far the body will go, and to perfect steps and combinations, dancers repeat movements over and over, sometimes for days. This puts a dancer at risk for repetitive motion injuries, especially if any joints are misaligned while the movement is being performed. Worse still, if the repeated movements are jumps or leaps, repeated impact can damage feet, ankles, and knees.

Neck and Shoulder Injuries

The majority of neck pain arises from neuromuscular tension, which is often a byproduct of movements in other parts of the body. Tension results in pain in the pectoralis minor, levator scapula, upper trapezius, or rhomboids. It also results in a limited range of motion for neck flexion, extension, inclination, and rotation. Neck tension can also affect shoulder mobility. Relaxation methods and strategic stretching are recommended to reduce tension and balance muscle strength so the head can be better supported.

Because most dancers concentrate on the muscles of the feet, legs, and torso, shoulder muscles are often under-conditioned, leading to injuries such as muscle spasm, tendonitis, bursitis, or even subluxation/dislocation. Moderate and severe injuries should be treated with rest, ice, and anti-inflammatory medication until moving is no longer painful. Then, proper stretching and muscular conditioning is recommended for rehabilitation or to avoid further injury.

Ankle and Knee Injuries

Dancers work in rélevé a great deal, and ballet dancers do so en pointe. Over time (especially with misalignment), these actions can compact the bones of the foot, destroy cartilage, and even cause hairline fractures or degenerative arthritis. Proper flooring, joint alignment, and muscular balance can help prevent these problems.

Ankle sprains are common. Immediate treatment should include extended rest and elevation, periodic applications of ice, and compression. Longer term rehabilitation involves gentle range of motion and strengthening exercises with extra support.

Shin splints often come from jumping on hard floors, and can be treated with rest, ice, and gentle stretching.

Common knee injuries and issues include tears in ligaments and cartilage, as well as inflammation of the fluid sacs and fat pads that cushion the knee. First response for these injuries is rest, ice, and anti-inflammatory medication, followed by properly strengthening the muscles to remedy the misalignment.

Proper warm-up and individualized conditioning can play an important role in preventing injury.

Sacroiliac Joint Dysfunction

The sacroiliac (S/I) joint, the pelvic junction where the ilium "floats" alongside the sacrum, transfers weight from the spine to the pelvis. Dysfunction can occur due to traumatic injury or repetitive forces over time, and commonly results from uneven leg length or pelvic misalignment due to tightness (or laxity) in surrounding muscles.

In cases of injury, 72 hours of the standard "Rest, Ice, Compression, Elevation" method of treatment is indicated. Anti-inflammatory medication to relieve swelling and pain is optional. Once this type of injury is confirmed, the individual should not move the affected area in any way that results in pain.

Once movement of the affected area is no longer painful, gentle strengthening, stretching, and range of motion exercises can be started to retrain the surrounding structures and encourage alignment that is more supportive. Pilates exercises are effective in providing necessary abdominal/core stabilization, and regular stretching of the psoas, quadriceps, hamstrings, and muscles attaching to the iliotibial band can even out imbalances in muscular tone.

Adolescent Stage of Development for Dance Education in Grades 8-12

High school students are mentally and physically capable of developing a regular exercise plan, and physically it is an opportune time to do so. The adolescent body is reaching maturity, approaching its peak functioning level without having had sufficient time and wear to begin sustaining the injuries almost always found in dancers. This time in a student's life is an especially good one to develop a plan of healthy eating, sufficient rest, and conditioning designed to address the dancer's individual flexibility, strength, and endurance needs, as well as any alignment issues.

Emotionally and mentally, this is a time when students are establishing identity, autonomy, and a world view, as well as displaying increased concentration and sophistication in both systematic and abstract thought. These conditions are ideal for exercises involving the composition, systematic revision, and verbal analysis of a dance, possibly ones related to a socially relevant theme.

Illustrating the Importance of Safety to Students

To address performance space safety, teachers can discuss the need to check backstage pathways and obstacles, stay out of the technicians' way during rehearsals, refrain from talking to the stage crew while working, and make sure the stage floors are swept before any class, rehearsal, or performance. Conducting a tour of a performance venue (if doing so is possible) is very useful for pointing out possible hazards.

Class and rehearsal space safety may be overlooked or forgotten because students spend so much time there, but teachers must emphasize safety procedures in these spaces for exactly that reason. Issues in the studio mostly relate to finding enough space to dance without colliding with other dancers. Students must be taught and reminded to cooperate with other students so that everyone can find adequate space at the barre or on the floor before each exercise. Students should use their peripheral vision and kinesthetic awareness to sense where other people are in the room, and to follow established entrance and exit pathways for across-the-floor exercises.

Encouraging Students to Make Healthy Lifestyle Choices

Students need guidance to learn and implement the main principles of a healthy lifestyle for dancers. These principles include appropriate eating habits, sufficient and consistent hydration, adequate rest, expansive lung capacity, release of neuromuscular tension, proper weight maintenance, and relaxation. Teachers should take advantage of opportunities to point out the individual benefits of each. During a class, for instance, the teacher might state that "Turns are easier when you've had enough sleep."

Teachers can emphasize the importance of healthy habits, but the requirements may be difficult for students experiencing the changes of puberty to meet. The stress of transitioning into young adulthood can lead teens to adopt unhealthy habits like foregoing sleep, behaving dangerously, smoking, using drugs, and drinking. Self-consciousness and body issues make teens especially vulnerable to eating disorders.

Frank classroom discussions can address choices, but may not always be optimal for addressing the difficult emotional situations in which teenagers often find themselves. One-on-one consultations may be called for when the teacher notices individual problems.

Developing and Implementing Individually Appropriate Conditioning Programs

Along with teaching technique, teachers also introduce students to fundamental concepts of the physiological conditioning required in order for students to maintain a body that is fit to dance. A teacher cannot overemphasize the importance of individualized conditioning to address a dancer's specific physical needs, minimize limitations and maximize capabilities, and produce a strong, flexible, coordinated, and versatile dancer.

If possible, a teacher should build a unit of study to address the different somatotypes and their individual needs into the curriculum. This unit can also familiarize students with the basic principles of proper alignment, common injuries and how to prevent them, and strategies for proper weight control. Teachers should cover the issue of eating disorders, which are common among dancers, especially teenagers and young adults. Every effort should be made to impress upon students the importance of physical conditioning outside technique classes.

High School Dance Education

Developing thought and movement skills centered on the awareness of one's own and other people's bodies and movements in time and space not only helps students understand themselves from the inside, but also helps them understand and better navigate the outside world. Skills related to this criterion include the assessment of internal ideas, thoughts, and emotions, as well as external environmental images and patterns that might be appropriate topics for dance exploration.

Implementation of this curriculum begins with exercises designed to foster a basic kinesthetic sense. These should be directed both internally and externally toward others and their potential movement choices. These exercises evolve into more finely calibrated internal perceptions, as well as more complex movement interactions with others. This curriculum also begins with the identification of external design cues for movement and the basic connections among emotions, ideas, and movement. It then advances into the identification of danceable images, details, and designs from a variety of environments.

Chapter Quiz

Ready to see how well you retained what you just read? Scan the QR code to go directly to the chapter quiz interface for this study guide. If you're using a computer, simply visit the online resources page at **mometrix.com/resources719/aepadance** and click the Chapter Quizzes link.

Creating and Analyzing Dance

Choreographic Ideas & Processes

Generating Choreographic Material

Some potential sources a choreographer can consult to help generate choreographic material include:

- **Visual Art, Architecture, and Design** → The visible products of someone else's creative urge are often inspiring to choreographers, who respond kinetically to form, line, space, and design.
- **Music** → Whether used as an actual accompaniment to movement or as pure inspiration, the formal elements of time, rhythm, and dynamics in music can often help the choreographer make movement choices that correspond to these elements.
- **Literature, History, Religion, Mythology, Folklore, and Fantasy** → All of these are sources for stories, characters, and situations that can be portrayed in dance.
- **Human Behavior and Interaction, Cultural Phenomena, etc.** → This is an ideal source because nothing is more fascinating to a human than watching the actions of fellow humans.
- **Psychological or Emotional States** → The drama inherent in the workings of the human mind and heart can often be expressed in interesting movements.
- **Patterns in Nature and Movement Phenomena** → Natural forms, movements, and rhythms are endlessly fascinating in their intricacy, variety, predictability, or unpredictability.

Creating Dance When There is No Specific Subject in Mind

Though many dances revolve around an overt theme—a unifying idea or intention that is specified (and often even researched) well before the development of choreography begins—others do not begin with a definite idea. These kinds of dances evolve out of movement play and improvisation by the choreographer in the studio.

When there is no established theme initially, a choreographer might spend an hour, a day, or a week in the studio alone, exploring, discarding, and keeping different movements. Through this attentive process of improvisation, bits and pieces of movement come together. Almost always, after enough time with them, an idea emerges that fits with the movements and ties them all together into a unified theme.

Coming up with a theme is imperative, as it provides direction for the development of further choreography. Once it is established, idea and movement tend to feed off each other, providing the intention for the piece.

Using Imagery to Develop Ideas

Once a central idea is established for a dance (or, just as often, even before the idea is fully developed), images accompanying that idea will likely begin to emerge during choreographic research. The choreographer pays attention to these images, recording and manipulating them, exploring the ways they can translate into or inform movement choices, and eventually using them to stimulate and generate choreography.

Since dance is an expressive form which seeks to communicate meaning through physical images and motion, it follows that using visual or emotional images ("soar like an eagle") to inform the choreographic and rehearsal processes, as opposed to abstract concepts ("embody the lift and thrust of flight") or clinical instructions ("elevate the arms, bring them down, and run with power") will naturally elicit strong images that will be reflected in the movement and its performance.

Improvisational Exploration and Choreographic Study

All choreography essentially begins with improvisation—trying out movements without knowing ahead of time what they will look or feel like, repeating or varying or discarding movements in the spirit of exploring and identifying ones that fit with the choreographer's mindset at the time. Improvisational exploration and choreographic study are related methods of focusing awareness and intention on movement in order to generate choreography.

Improvisational explorations begin with a set of suggestions designed to elicit movement—images to explore, questions to answer, kinesthetic input to pay attention to, tasks to complete, etc. They continue in a freeform style until the choreographer or dancer is able to glean some new direction from the movement.

Choreographic studies generally follow improvisational exercises. They focus and shape the kinesthetic/creative insights of raw movement exploration into more fully-developed movement phrases, each with a cohesive beginning, middle, and end.

Improvisation Skills Used to Explore and Generate Movement to Create Dances

Improvisation often proves to be a fruitful means of generating movement vocabulary and examining ways in which movement can be manipulated for the creation of dances. It can also serve as a way of expanding dancers' habitual patterns into more exploratory, spontaneous, and nuanced movement.

Unstructured, "free" improvisation—moving without premeditation and without any choreographic limitations placed upon the body or mind—can be a useful way to discover what that body and mind can produce.

Guided or structured improvisation exercises can also be effective. These exercises proceed from the idea that specific limitations can propel the resulting movement in surprising and useful directions. Any movement qualities or structural elements can be implemented as criteria for an exercise, singly or in combination. These qualities and elements include time, space, weight, energy, rhythm, flow, levels, direction, and speed, among others. In addition, improvisation exercise guidelines can include words or phrases, shapes, images, body parts, or tasks to be accomplished.

Changing Movement Quality to Manipulate and Shape Choreographic Material

Once basic movement material has been created and selected for a dance, it is subjected to crafting, shaping, and refining through the application of numerous choreographic devices. One of these methods involves the application of basic movement qualities—time, space, weight, and flow—through their various ranges.

For example, a choreographer could take a basic movement or two and change the amount of time it takes to do them: stretching them out over an entire minute, cramming them into a few seconds, or choosing various time intervals between the two. The movements could be varied in space, initiated with an indirect intention to land in an entirely new spot or finished with a decisive directness across the room from where they started. A previously light hop-and-skip movement could be imbued with additional weight, yielding a completely different impression. Or, an originally bound movement could be eased up to create a light and free flow.

Improvisational Exercises That Can Generate Choreographic Material for a Dance

Exploring shapes, body parts, or images is an especially useful starting point for improvisation. Possible initial instructions might be: "Choose two body parts to lead all your movements." Then, after some time with that idea, the following instructions might be given: "Choose a geometric shape, and let your chosen body parts lead you in tracing that shape's movement path along the floor." Other possible instructions could be: "Imagine that your goal is to move an object across the floor in as many ways as you can. Note how the object's size, weight, and texture affect its movement."

As improvisational exercises progress, students or choreographers should practice remembering, retaining, and repeating movements that grab their attention.

Once some raw, identifiable movement has been elicited, an exercise applying movement qualities and dynamics can often refine it into a choreographic study. Instructions for such exercises might be: "Repeat the body parts exercise, but with 10 times the weight as before," or, "Repeat the body parts exercise, but complete it in half the amount of time as before."

Contact Improvisation

In the contact improvisation form of modern dance, partners react spontaneously to each other's movements, often in close contact. Unfamiliar orientations of limbs and bodies are used. Contrary to ballet partnering, where one partner supports the other while both remain mostly upright, contact improvisation requires partners to distribute their collective weight to achieve, maintain, or transition through shapes and movements. This form allows partners to use each other as a support, ballast, launchpad, mat, ladder, blanket, etc.

Because contact improvisation is a mental moving exercise—practitioners are constantly learning to simultaneously balance the objectives of responding to movement, creating movement, and adjusting tempo, pressure, and expectations—it has proven useful for generating fresh choreography. Often, contact exercises will present a concept or task that aligns with the choreographer's intentions for a dance piece, and promising movement culled from the exercise will be repeated and manipulated to become set choreography.

Intention and Theme in the Process of Choreography

Central to the choreographic process is the intention for the dance—what does the choreographer wish to communicate to an audience, through what particular perspective will the information be communicated, and what is the purpose of communicating the information to the audience? The clearer the intention is in the creator's mind, the greater the chances that the resulting dance will be a cohesive, lucid expression.

If intention is the choreographer's initial question, theme is the method of expressing the answer. Themes can take almost any shape in a dance: investigations into pure movement combinations of space, time, and energy; emotional motivations; dramatic narratives; personality characterizations; dynamics of human interaction; or symbolic structures.

Intention does not always precede movement. Sometimes, the ideas don't emerge until movement "gets the mental juices flowing." Whichever the order of events, the choreographer uses the interplay between movement and the thoughts and emotions it elicits to focus and deliver the choreographic message of the dance.

Communicating Meaning Through Gesture and Movement

In the history of human development, movement predated language as a means of communication. Through eons of evolution, humans have become adept at communicating and understanding meanings and intentions conveyed through gesture and movement.

As an example, consider the three basic human gestures that we innately understand: the extension of a hand to be shaken or otherwise touched as a greeting; the turning of the head toward a sound or action, which indicates the focusing of attention (whether that focus is intentional or not); and the raised hand poised to strike, which communicates aggression.

For the most part, dancers are naturally attuned to the significance and meaning communicated by movement. This is true even of movements considered much "harder to read" than basic, pedestrian human gesturing. For that reason, dancers are especially adept at communicating through motion. Through sensitive perception and attentive portrayal by choreographers and dancers, audiences can "see" a myriad of meanings represented through dance.

Selecting Movement That Conveys Integrity and Meaning

In such an instinctive and sometimes mysterious medium as dance, the use of codified methods can seem foreign and even inappropriate. However, decades and even centuries of tradition have yielded wisdom about the creation of dance, wisdom that novice choreographers would do well to learn and apply.

One main choreographic rule of thumb is that solid, effective movement comes from "doing," not from "seeing." In other words, effective movement is movement that imparts a feeling of organic agreement with its intention and works well with the dancer performing it. It is not merely movement that looks pretty in a mirror. The latter, though sometimes pleasing to the eye, often results in movement that is flat, empty, or pointless.

Certainly, a mirror is useful for adjusting, manipulating, and refining movement once it is selected. During the initial stage of creating choreography, however, the gaze should be "turned inward," toward the creative impulse, rather than focused outward on how a movement looks.

Intention and Expression

Intention is found both in the overarching aspiration for the dance (the particular perspective that the choreographer hopes to communicate to the audience) and in each movement (the impression that each movement imparts). The degree to which movement intention is successfully conveyed is influenced by the partnership between the choreographer (who designs the movement) and the dancer (who must interpret and perform it).

Expression is the dancer's ability to convey movement intention through movements and facial gestures. Skilled dancers know that the angle of a dropped shoulder, how long a hand is pressed forward to say "stop," or even a look of inquisitiveness in the eyes can change the quality of an impression, whether the choreographer, dancer, or audience member is aware of it or not. The accuracy with which a dancer uses his or her body and face can support or undermine the overall impression the choreographer hopes to achieve.

Translating an Idea into a Fully Crafted Choreographic Work

The vast number of potential sources of ideas and inspiration for a dance can yield rich and compelling choreography, or a product that is flat, over-emotional, inane, or incomprehensible. The success of the endeavor depends on several factors related to the process of transforming an idea into a dance. These include:

- The chosen idea for a dance must be able to be expressed through physical actions. Some themes are too grand, abstract, or complex to be expressed through movement.
- The choreographer must present a particular perspective on the idea, rather than simply presenting it in its original form. All artists have something to say about their chosen subject, or they wouldn't have chosen it in the first place.
- A sufficient degree of choreographic craft must be imposed on the idea to save it from appearing half-baked, sentimental, or self-indulgent. It's important to keep in mind, however, that there are no guarantees this won't happen anyway.

Securing Musical Sources to Accompany a Dance

Musical accompaniment can contribute a strong element to a dance. Music (and how it will be used) should be given careful consideration.

Recorded music is easier and cheaper to access, and a greater variety exists now than ever before. Choreographers, however, still need to secure legal rights to use a musical piece for any professional performance outside a class or school recital. This can be as simple as contacting the publisher, providing details of the performance, and signing a contract for use. For short or small-scale engagements, the fee can often be waived.

For choreographers, opportunities for procuring live music can be limited because of budget, time or scheduling restrictions, or physical access to composers and musicians. In a scholastic setting, dance and music departments can often collaborate to provide access to live musicians. The choreographer should keep in mind that musical scores are also copyrighted. Therefore, rights must be secured to use them.

Choreographer Who "Has No Idea What to Dance About"

Under deadline to create a dance, an idea-less choreographer enters the studio and begins to move. Eventually, a combination of hops and a fall followed by a rise from the floor surfaces repeatedly. This reminds the choreographer of a traumatic hopscotch event from her childhood. She decides to portray the fateful incident in a stylized way.

She changes rhythms and retrogrades the original movements, expanding them into several phrases. Other movements begin to assert themselves in her body. She follows their lead, and soon a related but wholly different phrase has created itself, begging to be developed through the use of lateral shift and different instrumentation.

Realizing that she can heal some old wounds—while simultaneously entertaining an audience—with the proper compositional structure, the choreographer revisits the original theme, condensing and lightening it considerably. Then, after inserting thoughtful transitions between them, she sequences the original theme, the second theme, and the condensed original into a cohesive ABA' structure.

There Is No "One Way to Do It"

A choreographer begins with a vague idea of "flight." He watches birds, airplanes, insects, and even Superman movies. As he improvises movement in the studio, the idea becomes more clearly focused on the moment of lift-off and the sheer joy it brings. Now, his dance has an intention.

The choreographer's improvisational exercise focuses on elevating movement from middle level to high through leaps and lifts. As movements accumulate, the choreographer varies their size and tempo, changes their dynamics, and even asks other dancers to help him explore canon. Other exercises develop the movements into one phrase, then another, and then another. This continues until an identifiable theme emerges to express his "joyful lift-off" intention.

After experimenting with variations of his movement theme, which could include sleepy, terrified, confused, and elated, the choreographer chooses three and crafts transitions to move from the original theme to each variation. Thrilled that the dance conveys his original intention, the choreographer crafts an ending, finishing the dance.

Task-Oriented Improvisational Group Exercises

Task-oriented improvisational group exercises offer an excellent way for students to practice and develop the skills of critical thinking, creative problem solving, cooperation, and self-discipline. An exercise should present a task that cannot be accomplished by one dancer alone, but must be completed by several dancers working together in unconventional ways. The exercise should last long enough and be difficult enough to present an appropriate challenge (and be fun) without seeming impossible.

To conduct this type of exercise, the teacher divides the class into groups (3 to 7 students, depending on class size) and gives each group a task to be achieved (the same one for all groups, or different ones for each group). Examples of tasks may include: "Each dancer holds another dancer's foot in his or her hand, and the group crosses the floor without becoming unattached at any point" or "Dancers 'build' and then 'demolish' a building using only the bodies that are in contact with each other."

Critical Thinking, Creative Problem Solving, Cooperation, and Self-Discipline

Critical thinking, self-discipline, and written communication skills can be developed by consistently requiring each student to provide written analyses of class exercises. This also strengthens integration between the student's skills in spoken and movement languages.

Questions for students at all levels can focus on describing the structure of the exercise and the student's response while performing it; what the student thought the exercise's objectives were and whether he or she met them; what the student was "trying to say" with the movements he or she devised; and any images, shapes, movements, or phrases that stood out, as well as ideas, thoughts, emotions, or questions that entered the student's mind while doing the exercise.

These written analyses should be handed in to the teacher at every class meeting in order to develop critical and descriptive proficiency through repetition, and to instill a sense of accountability in students.

Providing Students with Opportunities to Think Critically and Creatively

Dance is a living art form. The optimal method of learning its components and practices is a dynamic one. Every abstract concept expressed verbally can also be illustrated by a movement or a dynamic visual or kinesthetic image. In this model, creative thinking is required to imagine and assemble the abstract, verbal, and kinesthetic components. Critical thinking is necessary to assess their appropriate associations and their proper application to each concept.

To develop creative thinking, teachers can ask students to supply their own imagery for particular movements. Students can string together movements to create a phrase for themselves and others to perform.

To develop critical thinking, teachers can call out the name of a movement and ask students to perform it (for younger students), ask students to supply the name of a movement or the concept illustrated by it, or show variations of or other ways a movement could be performed.

Developing Improvisational Skills

The development of new skills in dance, such as improvisation or choreography, requires a combination of talking and listening and doing and experiencing. Initially, teachers should verbally present the essential concepts for students to keep in mind while engaging in the practical improvisational exercises that follow. This information can be further assimilated during later discussion between the teacher and his or her students.

Improvisational exercises are often undertaken with a previously set or agreed-upon "score" in mind—a collection of defining boundaries or instructions to shape and direct the movement. This framework gives the teacher a perfect opportunity to use improvisational exercises to emphasize key features of the form, such as kinesthetic and spatial awareness, spontaneous movement choice, avoidance of self-censoring, and the implementation of choreographic concepts at appropriate points. In addition to setting the score beforehand, the teacher can call out guiding reminders and instructions to students during improvisations, and ask questions afterward that promote deeper inquiry.

Choreographic Devices, Form & Musicality

Elements of Choreography

- **Space** → This is the physical environment in which a dance is performed
- **Time** → This is the temporal structure within which a dance is performed
- **Energy** → This is the type and the amount of force applied to movement
- **Pattern** → Pattern refers to the recognizable, often repeated sequences in the space, time, and structure of a dance
- **Dynamics** → This is the interaction of the force, duration, and intention applied to movement, which results in a particular impression
- **Phrasing** → This is the time emphasis given to or withheld from certain movements within a phrase
- **Musicality** → This is a kinetic response to the rhythm, phrasing, and dynamics of music, which is expressed in the dance style
- **Expression** → This is the ability to communicate feelings, mental states, and more through both body gestures and facial expressions
- **Intention** → This is the idea or impression that a choreographer wishes to communicate with a movement
- **Context** → This is the atmosphere (political, cultural, historical, etc.) within which a dance is being presented
- **Structure/Forming** → This is the way in which elements of movement are arranged into sequences, phrases, combinations, and dances

Direction in Space

There is a human tendency to imbue movement in certain directions with corresponding connotations. **Forward movement** communicates assertiveness, **backward movement** communicates retreat, and **lateral movement** communicates concealment. To express ideas and images, dance uses directional movement to encourage these perceptions.

Certain areas of a stage are perceived as holding significance. Corners are "strong" spots, the upstage areas are associated with remoteness and grandeur, and the downstage areas are associated with personality and intimacy. And of course, "center stage" is viewed as the most captivating spot.

Naturally, paths between these stage areas will produce impressions of their own. A downstage cross from one side to the other is often used during comedic movements. An advance from upstage to downstage signifies confrontation. The upstage-right to downstage-left diagonal path is widely recognized as the one that creates the greatest impact, communicating everything from an epic journey to the arc of a personal relationship.

Pattern

Pattern can be generally defined as the choreographer's tool for synthesizing varied, dynamic, and interesting dances. It makes itself most readily apparent in the elements of space, time, and structure.

Pattern in terms of space is known as design, and encompasses many of the visual phenomena inherent to dance, such as shape, kinesphere, spatial path, level, direction, floor path, facing, etc.

Pattern in terms of time is most easily identified as rhythm, as in the pattern of accented and unaccented beats that repeat to create meter. Rhythmic patterns are as varied as the movements of a dancer's leg.

Pattern in terms of dance structure (or forming) appears in the sequencing and order of movements, phrases, and combinations. Sequencing patterns often successfully mirror natural rhythms, including rise/climax/fall, theme and variation, ABA, canon, rondo, etc.

Aspects of Time That Are Commonly Manipulated to Develop Choreography

- **Tempo** → Tempo is the speed of a movement or a movement sequence. It can be sped up to create intensity or excitement, and slowed down to impart languor or reluctance
- **Momentum** → Momentum the consistent increasing of tempo; it has a connection with energy (energy increases as the tempo speeds up, and decreases as it slows down)
- **Duration** → Duration is the amount of time a movement takes, from its initiation to its completion. Duration of inaction is the amount of time between ending one movement and beginning another
- **Rhythm/Accent/Meter** → Rhythm is a repeating pattern of beats, whether strong/stressed or weak/unstressed. Rhythmic patterns are combinations of weak and strong beats. Accents are beats with special emphasis placed upon them. Meter is the grouping of repeated, accented beats in a piece of music
- **Stillness** → Not only the absence of movement, stillness can also be understood as the absence of the flow of time

Choreographic Devices Used to Refine Movement for Choreographic Composition

Choreographic devices used to develop, manipulate, and refine movement for choreographic composition include:

- **Motif and Development** → Basic movements or short sequences are manipulated to create new but related movements.
- **Repetition** → Movements are repeated.
- **Fragmentation** → Part of a movement is performed.
- **Incorporation** → A movement is made part of another movement.
- **Accumulation** → More is added to the original movement.
- **Augmentation/Diminution** → The size of the movement is increased or decreased.
- **Tempo Acceleration/Deceleration** → The movement is speeded up or slowed down.
- **Rhythm** → The rhythmic pattern (not the speed) of the movement is varied.
- **Action/Reaction** → The original movement is the question, and the new movement is the answer.
- **Retrograde** → The movement is performed backwards.
- **Unison** → Multiple performers perform the movement in the same way at the same time.
- **Canon** → Multiple performers perform a movement in succession.
- **Instrumentation** → The movement is performed using a different body part.
- **Inversion/Lateral Shift** → The movement is performed upside down or using the other side of the body.
- **Quality** → The quality or dynamics of the movement is varied.
- **Level** → The movement is performed at a different level (levels are classified as high, mid, or low).
- **Staging** → The facing, direction, location, or floor pattern of the movement is changed.
- **Combination** → Any of the above strategies may be combined to develop, refine, or modify a movement.

Compositional Structure and Theme

Compositional structures are frameworks for the sequential pattern of a dance, such as ABAB, rondo, canon, or round. They help organize and configure the elements of a dance across time. A theme is a clear, non-repeating movement sequence, an expression of the dance's intention which, once established, can then be developed through variations.

In a theme and variation structure, the theme is first presented unadorned—hop-turn-step-leap-fall, for instance. Then, each variation gives the theme a different character without altering its original composition. (This is quite different from the choreographic device of motif and development, in which the sequence and even basic movements of the motif can be drastically changed by various development strategies.) Each variation expresses a different personality of the theme—playful, sluggish, distracted, etc.

The final outcome of a theme and variation structure will appear as a movement sequence repeated several times, each time with a different "face."

AB, ABA, and Rondo Structures in Composition

AB structure is a theme followed by a different theme. Although the two themes are different, they share a common element that serves to highlight their dissimilarities. A deliberate transition is beneficial for connecting Theme A to Theme B.

ABA form (sometimes written as ABA') is similar but returns to the first theme after finishing the second. Often, Theme A is repeated in a condensed or abbreviated form, which emphasizes the differences between the original two themes.

Rondo also makes use of the AB idea, but incorporates more themes in an ABACADA form, introducing more movement to contrast with the original theme. As with Theme B, each additional theme must have something in common with Theme A, as Theme A is referred to before each new theme is introduced. All of these forms are also used to organize structures in music.

Canon and Round Structures

In music as well as dance, the canon structure is used to vary the starting and ending time of a single repeated phrase (or parts of the phrase). This adds interest by combining the singularity of one phrase with the multiplicity of repetition. As a sequencing structure, canon can be used in many forms.

Reverting canons feature each dancer performing the entire phrase from beginning to end, but beginning at different times. These can be overlapping (one dancer begins before the previous one ends) or non-overlapping (each dancer waits for the previous one to finish before starting). A round is a type of canon that is reverting and overlapping.

In simultaneous canons, all performers begin at the same time, but at different starting points within the same phrase. In cumulative canons, dancers begin at different points in a phrase, "fall into step" as the phrase progresses, and end in unison.

Relationship Between Dance and Music, Sound, Spoken Word, and Silence

Aural accompaniment deeply colors an audience's perception of a dance. Choreographers must decide early in the composition process what effect they want to achieve with the accompanying sound.

Intertwined throughout history, music and dance have a strong affinity. Music can be performed live onstage, backstage, or in an orchestra pit (or even the audience). It can also be pre-recorded and played back. Choreographers should carefully examine music choices with prominent lyrical, rhythmic, or melodic features.

Now that technology has made sound engineering accessible, non-musical sound accompaniment can include any sound found on Earth. Sounds can range from one slight clang, to vocal sounds made by dancers or others, to a full-blown pre-recorded soundscape.

Spoken word (by dancers or others) can be a powerful accompaniment, but choreographers should beware of overwhelming a dance with words, especially poetry, narrative, or conversation.

Silence can create a deeply focused, intimate atmosphere or a stifling one.

Accompaniment for Different Types, Moods, and Intentions of Dance

One useful rule concerning accompaniment is to roughly correlate the number of sound producers (human voices, instruments, car horns in pre-recorded traffic, etc.) to the number of performers onstage. This will safeguard against overwhelming a single dancer with a massive cacophony or "underwhelming" a chorus of dancers with one lonely voice.

Choreographers also consider aesthetic similarities when choosing accompaniment. Ballet and classical music share defined structures and refined aesthetics. Jazz and popular music's improvisational styles fit with tap and jazz dance. Modern dance, the great experimenter, often uses unusual sounds and music.

Certain accompaniments are well-suited to certain contexts. Silence focuses audiences more intently on movement, requiring strong technique or compelling charisma from a dancer. Loud, fast music "sweeps up" an audience, so movement must be strong enough to "hold its ground."

Of course, a choreographer can choose to deliberately challenge these affinities if "shaking up" an audience's perception is the explicit goal.

Melody, Rhythm, Meter, Tempo, and Dynamics

Many musical elements—especially those involving time and structure, such as rhythm, meter, and tempo—have similar functions in relation to music composition and dance composition. The musical terms melody, rhythm, meter, tempo, and dynamics are defined below.

- **Melody** → This is a succession of tones set to a particular rhythm that serves as the "voice" in music.
- **Rhythm** → This is a repeating pattern of stressed and unstressed beats in a piece of music. Rhythm can exist cooperatively with or independently of melody.
- **Meter** → This is a repeated grouping of accented beats.
- **Tempo** → This is the speed at which music is played. Interplay between the respective tempos of movement and music is a powerful choreographic device.
- **Dynamics** → Defined specifically as the volume at which musical notes are played, dynamics also refers to the energy behind the playing and the varied time across which the music is played. In this way, dynamics in music are similar to dynamics in dance. Both give pieces variety and personality.

Rhythmic Patterns

Certain rhythmic patterns are prevalent in Western music and dance. Because dance is often taught to a standard 8-count, dancers' understanding of musical measure is often different than musicians'.

The **4/4 time signature**, also known as "common time," gets four beats per measure. Two measures equal a dancer's 8-count.

The **2/2 time signature** is also known as "cut time," as it cuts common time in half. There are two beats per measure, and 4 measures equal a dancer's 8-count.

The **3/4 time signature**, or "waltz time," is characterized by a strong-weak-weak beat pattern that reflects the down-up-up dance steps of a waltz. Two measures equal an 8-count.

Musicians and dancers begin counting differently. Musicians start counting on the 1 (as in "1 and 2 and..."). Dancers—who need time to prepare the body for its first movement—often begin counting on the "and" preceding the 1 (as in "and 1 and 2 ...").

Meter Signature

Meter is the repeated grouping of accented beats in music. Meter signatures (also called "time signatures") are written in music notation as a fraction. The denominator (bottom number) signifies the unit of measurement, the basic beat that makes up the rhythm. The numerator (top number) represents the number of these beats that make up one measure.

Most Western music is based on an even number of beats. Consequently, most time signatures have an even denominator (often 4 or 8, but sometimes 2 or 16) and an even numerator (most often 2, 4, 6, or 8). The 4/4 time signature is called "common time," and the shorter 2/2 signature is called "cut time."

Dancers in Western countries are attuned to this structure, resulting in the prevalent usage of the 8-count rhythmic bar by choreographers and teachers. (Who hasn't seen a choreographer portrayed as barking out "5-6-7-8!" to begin an exercise?)

Comparing the Use of Time (Tempo, Rhythm, Accent, Etc.) in Ballet and Tap

Usually choreographed with an existing work of music in mind, ballet closely reflects the rhythms of the western classical (symphonic) music to which it is most often performed. Balletic movement usually begins on the first count of a standard eight-count measure, makes use of multiple instrument voicings that correspond with the movements of different groups, and mimics note length to produce corresponding movement. Examples of the latter are repetitive changement jumps during eighth-note triplets and adagio extensions during whole-note legato sections.

In tap dance, the rhythm made by the feet upon the floor is paramount, whether the rhythm is in concert with or counter to the rhythm of the accompanying music, or the dance is performed a cappella, with no musical accompaniment at all. In keeping with tap's spirit of rhythmic play, tap dancers emphasize accent in their rhythms, and often employ syncopation to vary rhythmic patterns and keep things interesting.

Dynamics, Phrasing, and Musicality in Dance

Dynamics are a product of the interaction of force, time, and intention of movement. For every movement or phrase performed in a dance, the dancer faces an endless combination of choices about varying the degree of energy put into the movement and the time taken to initiate, sustain, or complete the movement. The dancer must also consider the choreographer's (and his/her own) aspirations for presenting a particular impression to the viewer. A split leap can be done lightly and quickly to give a playful impression, or very powerfully to make it appear quite spectacular to an audience.

A dancer can vary the time element while performing a movement phrase, performing some movements over a longer period of time and some over a shorter period of time. This produces phrasing. Musicality is phrasing in which the dancer visibly responds to the rhythm and dynamics of music. Both add to the "personality" of the phrase and, ideally, support the choreographer's intention for the movement.

Communicating Through Dance

Gestures (culturally meaningful movements of the limbs and head to express specific thoughts) and facial expressions are two major ways of communicating mood and intention in a dance. Mirroring and guessing game exercises are useful for helping students identify and reproduce effective gestures and expressions.

Dynamics (also sometimes called movement qualities) are the combinations of space, time, weight, flow, and effort that a dancer can vary to give their movements individual personality and color. Exercises exploring dynamics will require previous knowledge of combinations of movement qualities. Ideally, students will also have a knowledge of Laban's Effort Actions.

Exercises can establish one basic movement phrase, and then apply varying movement qualities ("gliding," "sharp," "heavy," etc.) in order to demonstrate different effects. Improvisational exercises that impose different movement qualities on spontaneous movements are also useful for discovering affinities (fast + direct = punch, or heavy + slow = drag) that produce specific impressions.

Developing a Sense of Timing and Rhythm

Students need to internalize movement patterns in relation to time, specifically the phrasing, sequencing, and rhythm of a dance.

Phrasing refers to the way in which a dancer performs the components of a movement at varying speeds. It can also refer to how a dancer performs movements within a phrase for varying lengths of time, changing the duration of movements from initiation to completion. Phrasing exercises can explore combinations of quick and slow, sustained and truncated movements.

Sequencing refers to when and in what order movements happen. Students can take turns performing the same movement or progression of movements in different orders or patterns of time, exploring canon, retrograde, etc.

Whether in movement itself or in relation to musical accompaniment, dancers must become attuned to rhythmic patterns, including ones incorporating pulse, beat, pattern, accent, and tempo. Exercises exploring these elements can easily be paired with music illustrating the concepts to facilitate easier assimilation and understanding.

Providing Students with Opportunities to Develop Their Choreography Skills

Choreography is a complex area with an extensive body of practices. Dancers must internalize these practices in order to apply them when creating dances.

Improvisational exercises are used in classes to generate raw movement that is later manipulated through the use of choreographic devices. After introducing the principles, uses, and objectives of each choreographic concept, the teacher can then facilitate exploration of these devices by having students apply one or two at a time to their own or other students' movement sequences. Students can then demonstrate their results for the class.

Verbal discussion can follow demonstrations, allowing students to analyze, compare, and evaluate the uses of different choreographic concepts in the various exercises. Some combinations will feel more fruitful than others, and students should have an opportunity to delve into the hows and whys of their perceptions. Discussions and exercises can be extended by having students prepare a written analysis of choreographic concepts and the insights gained from the exercises.

Analyzing & Evaluating Dance Works

Connection Between Dancers and Their Religious Entities

Historians agree that the earliest organized and recognizable dances arose out of spiritual beliefs and gratitude. People danced in thanks for the life, sustenance, shelter, or other bounty they had been given—whether by the earth itself, the Great Spirit that animated it, or particular gods that populated it.

In many cultures, it became common practice to dance until one reached an altered state of consciousness—through frenzy, dizziness, or exhaustion. Once in this state, the dancer could communicate directly with the intended deity. Today, many cultures still perform these types of dances as part of their spiritual practice.

A few examples of dances meant to establish a direct connection to the divine include: wildly abandoned Greek dances to Dionysus, the god of wine and dance; Haitian voodoo ceremonies in which dancers aim to become possessed by spirits; the repetitive spinning of Sufi whirling dervishes; and the trance-inducing Brazilian dances of Candomble, which are conducted to worship African Yoruba deities called orixas.

Goals of Historical/Cultural Heritage

Studying the significance of the cultural and historical context of dances helps students comprehend the universality and commonalities of the art form, and to increase their awareness and appreciation of various heritages and traditions, including their own. This results in more tolerant citizens with a more sophisticated understanding of the world and its cultures.

Implementation of this curriculum begins with a basic study of dances from various cultures and time periods. This may involve watching videos or films of past works. The characteristics of these dances and their cultural and/or historical significance should be discussed. Important historical figures in the field of dance should also be studied.

As students learn more, exercises involving more sophisticated identification, analysis, and comparison of a variety of dances can be completed. Eventually, this leads to learning and performing dances from various cultures and historical periods, and even reproducing or approximating choreography to deepen students' understanding of various dances.

Understanding and Analyzing Dance

Useful methods to understand dance include description, interpretation, appreciation, and evaluation.

- **Description** → Describing anything can help a viewer further understand what he or she saw. By paying attention to, and later describing, a dance's movements and images, audience members can enhance their conception and appreciation of it.
- **Interpretation** → The choreographer's objective is to express intentions through movement, without words. This leaves room for audience interpretation. Audiences can imagine and speculate about a choreographer's intentions, and can draw their own conclusions about meanings.
- **Appreciation** → Dance audiences can deepen their experiences by noting which aspects interested them or made them feel something, whether it was emotion, intellectual curiosity, or a physical sensation.
- **Evaluation** → Audiences can also discern the quality of both the choreography and its performance. Did the dance communicate its impressions (whatever they were) clearly? Did the dancers seem technically able, comfortable with the choreography, and well-rehearsed?

"Just the Parts in Front of One's Eyes"

Analyzing a dance's form is one way to process it in the brain. The visible, structural aspects of a dance's construction—the shapes and spatial paths of the movements themselves, as well as their placement in space, patterning, sequence in time, etc.—make up its form. These elements serve as the "words and sentences" in a dance's "vocabulary," and express the dance's message.

In order to examine these formal elements, audiences can consider such criteria as how and where the dancers moved in space, when they moved in time and sequence, whether the choreography presented clear and varied dynamics (changes in energy), if there were repeated sets of movements that underscored a certain image, etc.

Although these elements do nothing to address the intangible qualities that enliven a dance and give it character and excitement, they are useful building blocks to develop a basic understanding of a dance.

Dance Energy

The animating energy of a dance can be the most compelling of its elements, as energy provides clearer, more intuitively recognized "cues" to a viewer than a particular movement or any other formal element.

For example, any combination of steps across the floor can be performed with a strong, direct energy, which would communicate urgency, earnestness, or the sense of "being on a mission." The same combination of steps could also be done lightly with a free flow, which would communicate ease and possibly playfulness—a very different impression. The movements are the same, but the message is completely different.

Humans respond instinctively to energy, and can rely strongly on their own perceptions when considering its effects. In a dance context, this means that audience members can legitimately examine how the dance made them feel, what the accompanying images made them think about, and what overall impression they received.

Clues to Discern the Intentions and Quality of a Dance

Before a dance begins, audience members can look for clues about the dance or series of dances in the title. Is the title brief or wordy, descriptive or abstract? Audience members can also look at the program notes. Do they include quotes, highlighted information, or thank-yous to other choreographers who have created recognized works? The volume, style, and choice of pre-show music can be an indication of the choreographer's or the music or artistic director's tastes.

During the dance itself—in addition to the use of space, time, and energy in designing and arranging the movement—a viewer can look at the lighting plot. Are the colors warm or cool? Are the lights bright or dim? Does the lighting highlight particular parts of the stage? The viewer can also look at costumes. Do the dancers resemble someone or something? What colors, fabrics, and silhouettes are used? Finally, the viewer can study the staging. Are there set pieces? What do they look like? What do they do? Do the dancers follow a floor pattern or go to specific spots repeatedly? Where are the entrances and exits? Considering all of these elements will help a viewer get more out of the dance.

Putting a Choreographer's Work into Context

Artists, like all people, are influenced by environment, or context—styles, attitudes, peer groups, cultural habits, time period, and political events. They are also influenced by their place of origin, upbringing, education and training, philosophy, and past teachers and collaborators. These combine to shape the artist's work into a unique expression of his or her time, place, style, and culture. By keeping this in mind when looking at a choreographer's work, audiences can glean more information from a dance.

Once they are familiar with an artist's background and current work, audiences can also determine the influences that shaped a given dance. Styles come about as combinations of previous influences (as in the case of jazz dance arising from tap and social dance), or as deliberate rejections of them (as in modern dance reacting to ballet). Part of a choreographer's skill appears in the balance and restraint with which he or she pays homage to or rejects various influences.

Originality and Visual/Emotional Impact

Originality is a paramount quality for any artist's work. If audiences can walk down the street and see another work that is almost exactly the same, they're not likely to give it much attention. All artists are unique, with singular perspectives and backgrounds, and their art should reflect that.

Ideally, a dance should look and feel like no other. This can be a problem, especially within a small dance community or a single choreographer's canon. Many dances can look alike because they make use of the same stock movements and devices.

Visual impact (especially as a conduit to emotional impact) is extremely important in an art form whose images appear and then vanish in a moment's time. The lucky viewer will see a dance featuring images so striking that they won't leave his or her head, or the rare dance that imparts such a moving overall impression that he or she "can't shake the mood" it causes.

Formalistic Dance Piece

A choreographer may create a dance to explore the relationship between floor patterns and the directions dancers face, or to explore patterns in time created by combining long delays and short bursts of movement. The choreographer might even include "what happens if" scenarios that are based on chance.

In these dances, the space is quite visible in varying shapes made by bodies and the movements themselves, as well as levels, planes, facings, directions, and floor patterns in which the dancers move. Time can also be measured in the speed, duration, rhythms, arrangement, and sequencing of the movements. Choreographers can also explore dynamics by varying the weight put into the movements and the energy and timing with which the dancers approach, maintain, and release movements. Although abstract dances do not specifically aim to evoke viewers' emotions, they may still do so—and will certainly create impressions and elicit reactions of some kind.

Analyzing a Dance

Through the Eyes of a Choreographer

Choreographers, as the masterminds behind dances, see it all. They generally view performances through the lens of "what works and what doesn't," even once the dance is onstage in its final form. The finished product is always measured, voluntarily or involuntarily, against the original vision.

While watching a dance, the choreographer will almost certainly gauge the technicality and energetic effectiveness of the dancers' performance, and will make note of parts that may need to be adjusted for subsequent performances. Choreographers evaluate how well the accompanying production values (sound, lighting, etc.) work with the movements to articulate the overall vision. They may also choose to focus on the dance's formal elements, scrutinizing the staging in terms of levels, facings, directions of movement, areas of focus in floor patterns, etc., or the timing, pacing, and phrasing of the movements.

Through the Eyes of an Audience Member

Audience members can vary greatly in terms of their previous exposure to dance and other forms of art, their understanding of cultural expression, and their tolerance for the unfamiliar. All of these factors can affect their ability to analyze and evaluate a dance. There are, however, several characteristics that almost all audience members automatically use to assess a dance's value. These are as valid as any sophisticated cultural inquiry, and often overlap with the criteria uses by other assessors.

These points include: whether the dance holds the viewer's attention and is entertaining, whether it features technically proficient dancers, whether the music or other form of sound accompaniment works well with the movements, whether there are compelling images that can provides clues about the dance's "meaning," and whether the dance makes any clear point or lasting impression.

Through the Eyes of a Dancer

Dancers, consumed as they are (and must be) by constant training in technique, may tend to focus on a dance's technical elements and whether they were adequately performed when viewing a piece. If the dancer actually performed the dance in question, he or she may relive the dance entirely as a series of tasks to be achieved—this saut de basque combination which he nailed, that roll across the floor shooting up into the handstand which never seems to ascend to its full height, etc. Dancers are endlessly striving to improve their performance, so it is often difficult not to zero in on the moments that could have gone better.

Any dancer, whether participating in a performance or watching it, will likely be attuned to the choices made by the performers in terms of timing, phrasing, dynamics, movement quality, and energy. Dancers often take note of particularly effective movement phrases and look for them to be repeated or manipulated.

Through the Eyes of a Critic

Since a critic, by virtue of his or her occupation, sees many more dances than just about any other population (including dancers and choreographers), he or she is usually particularly well-informed about the cultural and historical context of a dance and its players.

Theoretically, the critic knows something about the choreographer's previous work; training and teaching lineage; peers and collaborators; current and historical political, social, and cultural working conditions; philosophy; and artistic focus and style. (The critic may be familiar with the dancers' backgrounds, as well.) The critic will look for a balance between continuity and inventiveness within this context, as well as the dance's relevance within the current cultural climate and community.

In addition to all of this, the critic evaluates all the same elements that the choreographer does: the integrity and strength of the dancers' technique, structural elements such as staging and timing, and whether the production elements are combined with the movements in a way that effectively expresses a clear vision and intention.

Lens of Genre

Every form of dance has signature characteristics that identify and define it—and that make it beautiful and distinct from all other forms. An audience member can look for these when watching particular styles of dance, and can then discern whether those characteristics are present and strongly represented.

For example, tap exemplifies rhythm and improvisation. If choreography ignores or contradicts the rhythm in an unpleasant way, or simply repeats time steps without ever choosing to improvise movements during the breaks, it could be considered an unsuccessful representation of its form. The same methods can be applied to evaluate modern dance's expressiveness and inquiry into creative movement types, ballet's fluidity and weightlessness, and flamenco's rhythm, passion, and footwork.

It should be noted, however, that working contrary to form does not necessarily make a dance "bad." Looking at form is simply a place to start when considering the elements and effects of a dance.

Evoking Particular Feelings or Reactions

Some dances are created to elicit an emotional response from audiences. They may represent characters, settings, or situations about which people already have strong feelings. For example, mythological stories have always been a favorite theme across many forms of dance, as the characters are strong, their defeats disheartening, and their triumphs inspiring.

Dances with a dramatic or comedic objective often borrow methods from theater, such as staging, costumes, props, and sets. These methods help set the tone for bringing forth certain feelings. In these dances, dancers often portray more emotion than usual through facial expression, gestures, and the particular kind of energy in their movements.

Whereas formalistic dances ask audiences to focus on the "what" and "how" of a dance, dramatic pieces draw the viewer into the humanity of the situation. They focus on the "why" or—in comedic pieces portraying the absurd behavior of a character—the "who."

Audience Member's Experience and Perspective

The performance of any dynamic (moving) work of art involves three essential parties: the choreographer, who creates; the dancers, who perform; and the audience member, who receives and interprets. It is important for audience members to understand that their own perspectives will color their responses to a dance every bit as much as anything the choreographer or dancers do.

Choreographers contribute intention, knowledge, and craft. Dancers supply their training, focus, interpretation, and energy. Viewers bring their own influential elements to a dance: past experiences; a sociopolitical orientation; aesthetic preferences; and a certain degree—or lack—of knowledge about dance in general and the specific choreographer, company, or presenting institution behind the dance.

As the saying goes, "We can only see what we can see." Differing combinations of the viewer characteristics mentioned above create a different version of the dance for every viewer, shaping perception more strongly than any choreographic intention.

Asking and Answering Questions

Many viewers leave a dance performance asking one main question: "What was that all about?" However, there are other questions audience members can ask and answer for themselves or other spectators that are slightly smaller in scope and more likely to conjure up bits of understanding. These include:

Did a clear message come through in the dance? What was that message? Did the dance tell a story, express feelings, solve a puzzle, comment on a situation, or just look pretty? Were there repeated movements or series that were easy to identify? Did specific images catch your attention? What images caught your attention, and what were they likely meant to express? What might the choreographer's intentions have been? What was the choreographer trying to say? Did the dance say it clearly? How did you feel after the dance? Can you distill the description of that feeling down to one sentence? Can you express that feeling using a single word?

Teaching Technique, Creativity & Performance Skills

Career Options for Dance Students

Dancers whose main livelihood is performing are usually extremely talented, and are very rare. Performing dancers work extremely hard, compete for scarce roles and spots in dance companies, get paid very poorly (especially in light of the toll their work takes on their bodies and career longevity), and often finish their performing careers at a relatively young age due to physical or financial concerns. However, if a student feels he or she is "born to dance," performing is an artistically satisfying route.

Working choreographers, who are paid to create choreography for dancers and companies, are even rarer than working dancers. They perform the work of a composer, a dancer, an agent, and an administrator. They must create the choreography, stay in good enough shape to demonstrate it, find and solicit companies and presenters who can and want to pay for choreography, and keep track of all the inherent scheduling, budgeting, and production demands.

The world of dance is indebted to great teachers. Many dancers, both performers and non-performers, choose careers in dance education, passing on their enthusiasm and knowledge to subsequent generations. Teaching options are numerous and more attainable than performance careers. Employers can include dance, theater, or physical education departments in public or private schools; private dance studios for students of all ages; and college dance departments.

Dancers with administrative skills can often use their familiarity with the special needs of dancers and the dance community to perform much-needed administrative work for dance companies, university dance departments, dance schools and studios, and performance venues. They may focus on areas such as fundraising, promotion, and company management.

Some dancers who have a knowledge of alternative movement forms and movement-based healing methods seek additional training to acquire certification for a career in dance therapy or other forms of movement study. These may include Feldenkrais, Alexander technique, Pilates, and others.

Developmental Stages of School-Aged Children Between the Ages of 5 and 12

Children Age 5-6 (Kindergarten, Grades 1 and 2):

- **Intellectual** → Counting, identification of colors, and vocabulary recognition
- **Emotional** → Self-assurance, capability, emerging responsibility and guilt, and pride in accomplishments
- **Social** → Cooperative play with children of the same sex and competitiveness
- **Physical** → Motor ability and control, skipping, hopping, jumping, and balancing

Children Age 7-9 (Grades 2, 3, 4, or 5):

- **Intellectual** → More sophisticated literacy and numeric skills, computer or musical instrument competency, and conversational ability
- **Social/emotional** → Increased confidence, independence, responsibility, moral consideration, humor, empathy, and an inclination to "belong"
- **Physical** → Increased coordination, muscle control, agility, stamina, and strength (may begin playing team sports and practicing physical skills for mastery)

Children Age 10-12 (Grades 5, 6, 7, or 8):

- **Intellectual** → More logical thinking, problem solving, abstract thinking, increased concentration and worry, sophisticated verbal skills, and a greater importance placed on popular culture
- **Social/emotional** → Growing need for independence along with a need for home and family stability, increased sexual awareness, and intensified peer influence
- **Physical** → Varies widely, but common developments are increased strength, agility, and fine and gross motor skills; body approaches puberty

Development of 8th to 12th-Grade Students

The high school years generally encompass the stage of puberty and the establishment of identity and a more solid world view. Specific forms of development include:

- **Intellectual** → Expansion of advanced reasoning skills (including hypothetical thinking, augmented logic capabilities, and the capability to make a decision by considering multiple options), abstract thinking skills, and meta-cognition skills (the ability to "think about thinking," empathize, project other's viewpoints, and think strategically)
- **Emotional/social** → Formation and establishment of a student's identity, independence, and autonomy, as well as greater intimacy, social skills, and sexuality (Many teenagers also seek leadership and inspiration as they begin to achieve and aspire to follow certain career paths.)
- **Physical** → Rapid gains in height and/or weight, development of sexual organs, body hair, onset of menstruation in girls, increase in glandular activity (sweat, oil, and acne), and continuation of brain development

Criteria for High School Dance Education

- Criteria for high school dance education include: perception, creative expression or performance, knowledge of historical or cultural heritage, and response/evaluation.
- Criteria for the development of perception skills develop a student's ability to exhibit kinesthetic and spatial awareness, and to perceive, understand, and synthesize emotions and ideas from the environment into movements.
- Creative expression and performance criteria ensure that students understand and apply principles of physical fitness and movement philosophy to the performance of dance, and also apply principles of composition and choreography when creating their own work.
- Historical or cultural heritage criteria assess a student's ability to recognize, understand, and reproduce various dance forms from around the globe and from periods throughout history.
- Response and evaluation criteria sharpen a student's perception of the form, characteristics, qualities, and uses of dance, and of the place of the art form in relation to other art forms and disciplines, and in society at large.

Goals of Creative Expression and Performance

The creative expression and performance component focuses on acquiring knowledge of essential physical concepts and implementing fundamental practices in three basic areas: making and keeping the body fit to dance, learning and practicing various styles of dance, and going through the process of making dance. Implementation of this component involves related but separate practices.

One practice involves the study of proper terminology for anatomy and movement, as well as concepts of—and conditioning practices for achieving and maintaining—alignment, strength, flexibility, balance, endurance, speed, and injury prevention.

Another practice aims to foster students' abilities to fully perform movement in many styles. In increasingly advanced exercises, students are taught movement; are then taught to memorize, repeat, and reverse it; and are finally taught to vary dynamics and make movement expressive.

In the final practice of this component, students learn basic compositional concepts and implement choreographic devices and compositional structures to create complete dances.

Developing a Student's Physical Skills and Performance of Movement

- **Mimicking** → The teacher performs the movement as the student watches, and the student then imitates the movement.
- **Movement repetition** → As students repeat a new movement, neural pathways and "muscle memory" are established, which help students recognize, reproduce, and refine the movement.
- **Visual cues** → The student collects information by watching the teacher and other students perform a movement, and then applies the information to his or her reflection in the mirror. This method is especially effective for visual learners.
- **Verbal cues** → While students perform a movement, the teacher observes and calls out suggestions for refining it. This method is especially effective for auditory learners.
- **Manual adjustment** → The teacher physically touches and repositions parts of students' bodies while they perform movement to give them a kinesthetic sense of the desired alignment, path, etc. This is especially effective for kinesthetic learners.
- **Imagery** → The teacher presents various images that illustrate and exemplify the desired shape, path, quality, or skill in a movement.

Organizing Lessons to Expand Students' Knowledge of Movement

A skilled teacher is able to analyze movements in terms of their difficulty and appropriateness for students' particular stage of learning. After demonstrating movement material to the class (and possibly accompanying the movement with verbal cues and dance terminology), the teacher may break the combination down into progressions.

In this method, the teacher addresses the mechanics of a movement or a phrase, first breaking down the actions of each of the body parts—feet and leg movements first, then arm and hand gestures, and finally torso and head movements—and allowing students to practice them separately before reassembling them into the whole movement. This method can then be applied to the next movement or phrase and added on to the first set. This process can be repeated for each subsequent movement or phrase until the student has learned the entire combination.

Performing Increasingly Complex Movements and Patterns

The whole-part presentation method has proven useful for teaching singular steps or short, simple sequences. First, the teacher performs the entire exercise while the students watch, and then breaks the movement down into parts, showing students a single movement and observing as they work to reproduce it.

In the part-whole-part presentation method, the teacher first points out and explains the particulars of any especially difficult parts before demonstrating the entire movement combination.

Then, as in the whole-part method, students work to perform the sequence while the teacher watches and offers feedback and assistance.

The add-on presentation method can be used to group movements into entire combinations. The teacher demonstrates the first part of the sequence, and the students reproduce it. When the students are ready, the teacher demonstrates the second part of the sequence. The students learn it, and then perform the first and second parts in sequence. This process is repeated to add on the third movement, the fourth movement, etc., until students have learned the entire combination.

Movement Skills and Elements for Students of Various Skill Levels

Movement for dance class must be challenging enough to keep students engaged in attempting and practicing it, but still simple enough to be mastered by all students in the class. This requires careful observation of each student's skills and implementation of movement at corresponding levels of difficulty.

In any class, there will be students who progress more slowly when learning and reproducing movement. Students who require more practice than others to master new movements should be treated with patience and understanding, and should be encouraged when they achieve partial successes as they progress.

Slower learners can be accommodated without impeding the progress of the entire class. Often, more advanced students will enjoy having time to repeat and refine skills once they've acquired them, which will give the teacher time to work with students who need additional assistance.

Teaching Movement to Students Who Learn at Different Paces

The inclusive style of teaching invites dancers to select the level of difficulty at which they will perform a given exercise. The teacher presents a medium level movement combination, and then varies the difficulty of a number of aspects of the movement, including speed, complexity, number of turns, addition of beats or jumps, use of rélevé or fondu, directional change, etc.

Students who wish to focus on the basics or those who learn combinations more slowly can choose to perform the combination at half the regular speed, on full foot instead of in rélevé, without jumps, with single turns, etc. Students who are more advanced or those who wish to push themselves can choose to perform the combination at a faster speed or incorporate added beats, more revolutions, directional changes, etc. Teachers may also apply any of these options to selected students in the interest of developing a particular skill.

Helping Students Employ Appropriate and Effective Imagery

Imagery can be used as verbal cues to help dancers clarify and organize their thoughts and perceptions about body positioning during stasis and movement.

Kinesthetic images, which evoke sensations in particular body parts to achieve a corresponding position or shape, are naturally useful for calling a student's attention to how a movement "feels from the inside." For example, the kinesthetic image for a parallel side bend might be: "Feel the stretch along the side of the body, from outside the heel all the way up to the outside of the leg, hip, ribs, under the shoulder girdle, and through the top of the head."

Anatomical images focus on the structure of the body, and are therefore perfect for enhancing dancers' mental conceptions of alignment and translating them into properly applied muscle contraction to achieve correct posture. For example, an anatomical image given while students are standing in parallel might be: "Engage the arches of the feet as though there were a bubble of air under each."

Imagery stimulates dancers' imaginations and emotions, connecting their bodies to their hearts and minds, and animating their movements with purpose and vitality.

Visual images are especially useful for enhancing technique, as teachers can choose images with shapes similar to the desired body shape or spatial path. Examples of visual images might include: "Fall forward like a board, stiff from head to toe," or, "Développé like there's a balloon attached to your toes—rising, rising, rising effortlessly."

Pictorial images, which evoke an entire mental scene, can focus or transform performance qualities dramatically. These mental pictures are often associated with particular feelings or qualities, internalized by the dancer, and immediately translated into movement that exemplifies and exudes the associated feelings. For example, the pictorial image "Glide like a crane landing on a still lake" conveys movement with focus, tranquility, and a natural majesty. In this way, imagery can help dancers use movements to convey an idea, thought, or emotion.

Enhancing Teaching and Learning in Dance

Considering the volume of information to be transmitted in the field of dance, constant verbal discussion and live interaction are crucial in the classroom. Instructional books abound, and vary in terms of their effectiveness.

Besides live performance, film and video are the most visible and direct ways to transmit dance, although using video as a means for dancers to see and reproduce choreography has traditionally had its limitations. Video websites like YouTube, Daily Motion, and others provide access to endless choreography, but the level of performance skill varies widely. If these sites are used, dances should be considered and chosen carefully.

Increasingly, interactive dance DVDs are available that are designed not only to help dancers enhance their skills, but also learn and reproduce particular choreography. This process is made dramatically easier by standard features such as pause, slow motion, and frame-by-frame capabilities. Extra features, such as floor pattern maps, variable camera angles, split screens, looping options, text descriptions, time codes, and accompanying musical tracks may also be available.

Making Use of Community Resources and Support

Because dance is traditionally chronically underfunded, it is endlessly important for dancers to be able to utilize many different forms of support whenever possible. This is a survival skill for many dancers, and should be taught alongside other skills.

Teachers can introduce and advocate partnerships between dancers in the school program and entities in the school's municipal community. Assuming school regulations permit "booster organizations," local businesses could be solicited to volunteer, provide donations or sponsorship, or run advertisements in performance programs. Recreation centers could be asked to donate space and gym and/or studio time, or to lend equipment.

The students' dance community should also be seen as a source of support. Members of this community include fellow dancers, teachers, counselors, staff, administrators, and parents. These are the people who offer rides to workshops and auditions, set up chairs, work the box office, hand out programs, and work as stage crew members during performances.

Chapter Quiz

Ready to see how well you retained what you just read? Scan the QR code to go directly to the chapter quiz interface for this study guide. If you're using a computer, simply visit the online resources page at **mometrix.com/resources719/aepadance** and click the Chapter Quizzes link.

The History and Roles of Dance

Dance in Cultural Contexts

Context

Context helps determine whether intention is clearly communicated to the audience. It is impossible to escape the atmosphere in which a dance is presented. Choreographers need to consider the town (sometimes even the neighborhood), country, time period, audience demographics and cultural subtexts, historical and current events, and the political and artistic climate in which they are presenting their work.

Ignorance or miscalculation in this area can get work booed, snubbed, or banned. What seems like a funny, if grossly overstated, characterization in one theater can seem like an insultingly spot-on portrait to audiences in another. If the choreographer's intention is to provoke or to illuminate a social issue, this effect may be a desirable one. Otherwise, choreographers should use caution.

Understanding the Cultural Context

Cultural context—the time, place, cultural climate, and artistic influences surrounding artists and their work—can provide a strong set of clues to a viewer trying to analyze a dance or canon of work, and can be understood by using several methods.

Comparing and contrasting a dance with other dances from the same time period—whether works made by the choreographer in question or several different choreographers—can give a clear "snapshot" of a certain era, especially if it is or was defined by particular historical or political events.

Comparing and contrasting a dance with other forms of art from the same time period can provide an even clearer picture of the cultural climate of the time.

Comparing and contrasting a dance with earlier works by the same choreographer can illustrate the development of the artist's canon throughout his or her career.

Historical Role of Dance in Human Communities

For as long as the customs of different cultures have been recorded, dance has been vitally important in identifying and communicating ideas about environments, living arrangements, social standards, and the ideals and spirituality of a people. Before language and music were created by early humans, people were telling stories with movement—acting out for each other the events of the day's hunt, lifting their hands joyously to greet a much-needed rainstorm, or raising a protective arm to shield a child from danger. These movements, understood through a shared set of experiences, became the earliest basis for dance.

Once ideas of spirituality took shape in the cultures of ancient peoples, dance was there to accommodate and communicate those concepts, too. Clasped hands and bowed heads or upturned faces and upraised arms—the standard postures and gestures of many world religions—communicate the gratitude, supplication, reverence, and worship involved in spiritual practice.

Traditional Dance Practiced by Different Cultures Throughout the World

"Folk dance" is a catch-all term for any traditional dance participated in communally by non-professionals. Worldwide, these dances can be placed into two main categories: religious dance and social dance. Both are an effective way of transmitting culture and reinforcing a people's communal values and experiences.

Religious dances reflect a people's spiritual beliefs. They include storytelling dances to transfer knowledge, medicine dances for healing or protection, imitation dances (mimicking important animals or events), commemorative dances demarcating annual events (solstices, harvests, animal migrations, etc.) or personal landmarks in individuals' lives (birth, initiation, marriage, death, etc.), and dances to achieve a spiritual connection with deities.

Social dances are primarily for recreation and community. They include work dances (mimicking movements of a particular kind of labor); courtship dances (less prevalent in cultures that impose strict limitations on contact between the sexes); war dances to prepare, motivate, or intimidate before battle; and communal dances to enhance cooperation.

Court Dance and Sacred Dance

The aims of court dance and many forms of sacred dance are similar: to celebrate and show respect and devotion to a ruler, or to a deity, ancestor, or other spiritual being. Often, the two styles of dance are most similar in cultures where political leaders are also spiritual leaders. (These dance styles differ from ecstatic religious dances, where the goal is to work dancers into a trance believed to facilitate a direct connection with the divine.)

These two forms share an overall atmosphere of circumspection and decorum and are performed at a stately pace with serene movements. This conveys an attitude of deference from the dancers, communicating respect and acknowledging the power of the leader or god (or both) that the dance is intended to honor. The dances are also visual spectacles, often incorporating costuming elements or environmental adornment such as shrines and offerings. In court dances, predictability and tradition are prized over invention.

Native North American and African Dances

Dance forms practiced by many Native American nations within North America and by traditional African cultures share not only cultural and spiritual motivations, but also movements.

Numerous Native American and African dances are designed to bring the dancer closer to their god or gods through worship, exaltation, gratitude, imitation, or trance. Other dances depict animals, plants, and other natural forms the dancers encounter and depend upon in daily life.

The basic posture of both African and Native American dance is an upright position with a slight tilt forward at the waist. The knees are usually bent. Rhythms are created by repeated stamping movements that help the dancers locomote in a circle or sometimes in a forward-and-backward moving line.

The two styles diverge in their use of the spine and arms. Upper-body movements of African dance are much larger and freer, while in Native American dance the spine is mostly kept straight and the arms are held low.

Neighboring Countries Whose Traditional Dances Are Similar

While folk dances vary within countries from region to region, the types of folk dances found in different countries can also share basic elements as a result of people migrating to and from neighboring countries.

For example, the dances of many Balkan countries such as Albania and Macedonia resemble styles also seen in neighboring Greece. Dancers bounce rhythmically in a snaking line, often with a lead dancer performing special tricks and jumps.

Partner dancing in Europe traveled around the globe, wherever British, French, and German colonists went. In South American countries, the dances were paired with traditional Latin rhythms, and promptly traveled northward to take over US dance floors in the 1930s and 1940s.

As global travel and our interconnectedness due to the Internet continue to increase and accelerate, influences from unlikely, far-flung countries have begun to appear in the dance and culture of other countries. This can be seen in the recent Balkan-Beats and Bollywood influences in DJ and social dance culture in the United States.

Banning of Traditional Dance

Colonizing governments often seek to suppress traditional dance as one method of gaining dominance over a people. Religious officials also ban them for reasons of supposed immorality. Dances, if not wiped out entirely, often transform from spiritual practices into social or performance dances.

Native North American dances, outlawed by the US government in the late 19th and early 20th centuries, have been somewhat preserved and perpetuated by the decision of tribal elders to transform traditional powwows into dance-centered competitions. A similar phenomenon happened in Hawaii, where some dances became purely tourist attractions, while others retained their spiritual significance.

In India in the early 20th century, the government outlawed the existence of devadasi, young girls whose lives were dedicated to learning classical dance for the purpose of serving particular deities. Brahmin families established schools to propagate bharatanatyam, kathakali, and other forms, which now flourish in India and abroad.

Using Dance to Gain Power Over Subjects

The phenomenon of court dance developed within the monarchies that existed throughout history and around the globe. The original purpose of court dance was to please the royals with beautiful dancing, which they either joined in with or watched and commented on.

Displays of special skills by dancers served two purposes: to delight spectators' senses, and to attest to the wealth and power of the monarch who could afford such skillful dancers. Dance represented another opportunity to improve a ruler's reputation through a display of power and wealth.

Court dance was also used to inspire allegiance in subjects and followers. The reasoning behind this use of court dance was that any country whose courts featured such skillful dancers would certainly invoke pride and patriotic feeling in its citizens. A perfect example of this can be seen in the thousands of synchronized dancers and gymnasts who perform in the North Korean Mass Games, a massive pageant of nationalistic unity.

Dance as an Explicit Language

Dance, an expressive art, has a natural affinity with language. When studying dance, we speak of a set of movements as the "vocabulary" of a dance. In some cultures, dance has long been used to communicate very specific ideas and stories through a dancer's images and expressions. This is especially evident in Hawaiian hula and in forms of Indian classical dance, which both have thousands of hand gestures signifying specific words.

As certain cultures have historically sought to colonize or enslave others, they have consistently worked to suppress the native language of those they wished to conquer. As a result, subjugated peoples have sometimes turned to dance as their "secret language." For example, when African slaves in the United States were forbidden to speak their native languages or sing traditional songs, they often used dance to communicate in a secret language the "masters" could not understand. (Eventually, dance was banned too.)

World and Social Dance

Many social dances around the globe are thousands of years old, having developed naturally from the particular landscape, kinds of work, spiritual needs, sociopolitical position, and community-wide culture of their peoples.

Sometimes, these forms remain unchanged, and are preserved by their originating populations. Sometimes, they are affected by outside influences from other parts of the world. The advent of folk festivals has helped preserve the native traditional dances of various countries, but in other places where culture has been demolished by war, land development, or other catastrophes, the dances are lost as the people are scattered.

However, as global communication becomes more available and global travel more accessible, some subcultures of various countries learn about and adopt the dance forms of others. These dances are thereby preserved in a completely new context. The phenomenon of rugby players performing Maori haka chants and dances before a match is a good example.

Ways in Which Dance Forms Interact

Hybridization of dance happens as dancers continually seek to improve and expand their training by taking classes in numerous styles. Once a dancer "gets a movement in his or her body," it becomes part of the dancer's movement vocabulary. During the creative process of choreography, movements from all styles in which the dancer is proficient can be combined in a myriad of ways.

This permeability of form has always existed in dance. Similar dance moves can be found in different countries, and modern dance choreographers work with ballet companies (and vice versa). Today, because electronic communication and easier international travel offer greater access to global dance forms, they spread into more varied communities faster than ever before. This increases the number of salsa, African, tango, hip hop, swing, hula, baile folklórico, and other classes in a community, and results in more versatile dancers.

Global History of Dance & Influential Figures

Classical Dances of Asian Countries

Classical dance forms in many Asian countries, including India, Indonesia, Java, Cambodia, Thailand, and others are similar in terms of purpose, movement, costuming, and other elements.

Often, the purpose of classical dance forms is to exalt a deity or depict a mythological or cultural story. Exacting combinations of carefully prescribed finger, hand, foot, and head positions and movements, as well as eye and facial expressions are enhanced by elaborate costumes, headdresses, and masks. The latter three elements are often used to depict the gods or their servants.

Reasons for these similarities include the age of the dance form, the proximity of the countries to each other, and migration patterns. The older a dance form, the more opportunity other cultures have to learn and adapt it. Many forms of Asian dance are thousands of years old, and have had plenty of time to "travel." The proximity of the countries to each other and migration patterns also make it more likely that travelers, students, and immigrants will transmit the form from one country to another.

Indian Classical Dance

Dance has enjoyed a respected place in Indian culture, with deities such as Lord Krishna portrayed in dance. Most forms of Indian classical dance can trace their roots back to the Sanskrit text Natyasastra, which codifies elements of classical dance, including mudras (hand positions), foot patterns and gait, and limb positioning. Through the 9th century BC, dances stayed mainly within the confines laid out by this text.

After this period, classical dance began to diversify according to regional influences, and to deviate from the Natyasastra's principles. During this time, the individual styles of bharatanatyam, kathak, orissi, kathakali, and manipuri began to take shape.

Widespread practice of Indian classical dance began dying out during British rule. In the early part of the 20th century, however, a concerted effort by those interested in dance and culture led to a revival and the establishment of dance schools to preserve India's dance traditions.

Birth of Ballet

During the Italian Renaissance, dancing was done by the royal court to please the monarchs (who also participated in the dance). Catherine de Medici, an Italian noblewoman and patron of the arts, married King Henry II of France in the mid-1500s. She brought with her the Italian court's dancing master, Balthasar de Beaujoyeux. He choreographed what is considered the first true ballet: Ballet Comique de la Reine.

A century later, King Louis XIV advocated for the form, requiring his courtiers to participate in ballets, and even training and performing in them himself. (He got the name "The Sun King" from the Ballet de Nuit, in which he performed.) In 1661, he

established the Académie Royale de la Danse with Pierre Beauchamp as director to codify the language, rules, and defining concepts of ballet, such as turnout and the five foot positions. These are still taught today.

Ballet arose out of court dance during the Italian Renaissance in the 16th century. It spread to France through art patron Catherine de Medici, who brought her dancing master and musicians with her in the mid-1500s when she married King Henry II of France. Ballet caught on in France over the next century, finding its greatest favor with King Louis XIV. This monarch established the Académie Royale de Danse, the first official school of ballet.

From there, ballet spread out geographically in all directions. Schools and performing companies were established in many countries, including: Russia (the Vaganova method taught at the Russian Imperial Ballet School and Sergei Diaghilev's Ballet Russes being two of the most famous), Italy (Enrico Cecchetti developed a strong and fluid style), England (the Royal Academy of Dance), France (l'École Française), Denmark (the Bournonville school of the Royal Danish Ballet), and the United States (George Balanchine's New York City Ballet).

Ballet

The earliest forms of ballet were developed in Italian and French courts. Over time, ballet transformed into—and remains today—a rarefied form of concert dance performed by highly trained individuals. Posturally, it is distinguished by a lifted and contracted torso, leg positions that are turned out from the hip, and upright balances upon the feet (often upon the tips of the toes).

Aiming for a sense of effortlessness and weightlessness, ballet movements are generally approached with a sense of elevation and elongation of the dancer's silhouette. The same basic movements are taught to children and practiced daily by veterans.

Reflecting its courtly origins, ballet has maintained a refined and rarefied aesthetic, often depicting romanticized versions of nature, fairy tales, and unrequited love. These are especially well-expressed by the classic ballet tradition of the pas de deux, a duet between a male and a female dancer in which the male dancer guides, steadies, and lifts the female dancer in extraordinary movements.

Couple Dancing

Two partners dance in close contact, facing each other, hand-in-hand or in a formal embrace. This familiar example of "couple dancing" is a Western European concept. It is one that is not accepted by many cultures around the globe, especially where arranged marriages are the norm and rules of contact between the sexes are strict. These types of cultures include many Asian, Native American, and African ones.

European post-medieval court dances began to feature a man and a woman dancing in close contact. By the mid-17th century, couple dancing moved from the courts to the middle and lower classes with the burgeoning popularity of the waltz. The common forms of ballroom dancing evolved from this tradition, and it remained a standard of social dancing in Western society for centuries.

Couple dancing underwent a fundamental change in form in the 1960s, when partners began dancing together on a dance floor without touching each other.

Tango

Tango originated in lower-class neighborhoods in Uruguay and Buenos Aires, Argentina. In the early 19th century, thousands of European men migrated to this developing Spanish outpost to find work, bringing the new European configuration of partner dancing—and few precious women to dance with—with them.

Brothels were popular, and while-you-wait entertainment was provided by musicians playing the mix of European instrumentation, flamenco and minuet timing, and African rhythms that would become tango music. Outside the brothels, dancing skill became extremely important for attracting a scarce mate. In this intensely focused environment, tango was born.

By the early 20th century, the form began to travel with sailors, dancers, and musicians. In Paris, it caught fire and spread across Europe, eventually coming to the United States around 1913. When tango achieved international fame, the upper classes in Argentina claimed it as their own. Now, the form is popular around the world.

Slavery and the Origins of Many Quintessentially American Dance Forms

It can be argued that without the tragedy of slavery in its historical record, the United States would not have spawned many of the art forms now considered essentially American, including blues music, rock and roll, tap dance, jazz dance, swing dance, breakdance, and hip hop.

While the immigration of people from Africa to America would certainly have happened at some point even if slavery had never existed (as a result of normal global migration patterns throughout history), it would likely not have happened early enough or on a large enough scale to affect American culture as it did.

African dance and musical elements lie at the heart of all the forms of music and dance mentioned above. Key defining elements of these African influences are the use of color symbolism, incorporation of rhythmic patterns, and integration of humor and improvisation. African music often emphasized rhythm over particular melodies, and allows for mimicry and embellishment in repeated parts, allowing for a great deal of variety. These elements are what give the forms their distinctive fire and variety. These elements, combined with all the other cultural influences of the US melting pot, define American art forms.

Cultural Developments That Gave Rise to Modern Dance in America

At the end of the 19th century, the world was changing faster and faster. The second Industrial Revolution was transforming the way people worked and lived, and this brought about a corresponding cultural change in Europe and in North America.

Artists and writers were setting aside conventional methods of expression in favor of new ideas. In this atmosphere, Loie Fuller, Isadora Duncan, and Ruth St. Denis began forging their own individual movement styles and laying the groundwork for what would become modern dance.

After the unprecedented horrors of World War I in the early 20th century, Americans were ready to forget and move forward with speed, gaiety, and new forms of art and entertainment. The Denishawn School, established during this time, produced Martha Graham, Doris Humphrey, and Charles Weidman. These were the dancers who would capitalize on the freedom of the Roaring Twenties to create the new form of "modern" dance.

Educational Festivals of Modern Dance in the United States

One major development that established modern dance as a legitimate artistic tradition in the United States was the founding of educational festivals. These events offer classes, performances, and community—as well as choreographing and performing opportunities—for students, emerging dancers, and established artists alike.

In 1933, after the closure of the Denishawn School, Ted Shawn established a summer dance festival on his family farm in Jacob's Pillow in upstate New York. This festival is still held today.

The Bennington Summer Dance Festival in Vermont, which was held from 1934 to 1942, was originally staffed by Martha Graham, Doris Humphrey, Charles Weidman, and Hanya Holm. The festival was a precursor to today's American Dance Festival. The American Dance Festival moved to Connecticut in 1947, and then to Duke University in North Carolina in 1978.

Considerably newer but still considered "one of the Big Three," the Bates Dance Festival was established in 1983 at Bates College in Maine.

Butoh

The profound destruction of World War II gave rise to a generation of Japanese artists whose work responded to the devastation in unconventional ways, challenging previous societal notions of art, authority, and propriety. The movement performance form of butoh was originally developed by two artists: Kazuo Ohno and Tatsumi Hijikata. They were influenced by their earlier studies of

German expressionist dance, and began creating work that established the butoh style around 1959.

Butoh relies heavily upon imagery (overt or obscure) and normally employs slow, controlled movements that can contort the performer into grotesque shapes. The form is frequently presented in extreme environments, and often addresses taboo topics. Butoh shares a number of characteristics with modern dance. Each was a response to older, restrictive dance traditions. Additionally, each form encompasses a wide range of natural, philosophical, and formal approaches that are often devised by practitioners. However, each style has an easily recognizable and identifiable form.

Modern/Contemporary Dance

Modern dance began in America at the turn of the 20th century with the innovations of Loie Fuller, Isadora Duncan, and Ruth St. Denis. All of these dancers were reacting against the rigidity of ballet and searching for a natural, authentic movement form. St. Denis married dancer Ted Shawn and opened the Denishawn dance school in 1915.

In the 1920s, Denishawn students Doris Humphrey, Charles Weidman, and Martha Graham, along with west coast dancer Lester Horton, became the pillars of the modern dance form. These dancers created their own distinct styles, each of which is taught as basic technique to contemporary dancers today.

Subsequent dancers further expanded modern dance technique. These dancers included Jose Limón, Alvin Ailey, Paul Taylor, Katherine Dunham, and Merce Cunningham, who revolutionized the form with his abstract approach. After them, the Judson Church and other post-modernist artists in the 1960s and 1970s further expanded the idea of what dance could be.

Tap and Jazz Dance

British Isles and Irish immigrants brought along their native forms of dance, many of which required shoes with metal taps designed to amplify the rhythmic stepping sounds. During the mid-19th century, white performers in American minstrel shows began presenting these dances along with the dances of African slaves found in the American South. Shortly after, black performers began doing the same. The two

forms merged into tap dance, which gained popularity during the vaudeville era and the 1940s and 1950s in Hollywood. Tap then fell out of favor for many years, but experienced a resurgence in the 1980s.

Jazz dance took significant influence from from tap as it emerged in the 1940s. It kept the original improvisatory style, but abandoned the taps on the shoes and added stylization from African, Caribbean, and African American forms, as well as ballet and other styles. Jazz gained supremacy in New York's Broadway productions and in Hollywood movies, and spawned a whole new movement: hip hop dance.

Breakdancing and Hip Hop

Tap dance arose from traditional Irish and African dances, and jazz dance in America arose from tap. Less than a century later, another combination of forces resulted in a new dance form. First funk and then hip hop music produced a form of social dance known as breakdancing. This dance style developed alongside other skills of the hip hop culture, such as rapping, DJ'ing, and graffiti.

Originally, hip hop dance consisted of breaking (influenced by the dances of James Brown, martial arts, and gymnastics), locking, and popping. As breaking grew past its early stages, it accumulated more innovative styles from other areas, such as funk styles from the west coast.

Eventually, hip hop became a distinct movement form of its own, even spawning a subset of jazz dance with basic movement vocabulary that was taught in classes and used to develop choreography.

Contributing Individuals to Ballet

- **Catherine de Medici** → She brought the precursors of ballet to France in the 1500s.
- **King Louis XIV of France** → He established the first ballet school in France in the 1600s.
- **Pierre Beauchamps and Jean-Georges Noverre** → They codified many standard ballet rules still used today.
- **Agrippina Vaganova, Enrico Cecchetti, August Bournonville, and Alicia Alonzo** → These teachers established and disseminated the distinctive ballet styles of Russia, Italy, Denmark, and Cuba, respectively.
- **Marius Petipa** → He was the creator of legendary ballets for the Russian Imperial Theatre, including "The Nutcracker" and "Swan Lake."
- **Sergei Diaghilev** → He was the founder of Ballets Russes.
- **Mikhail (Michel) Fokine** → He was the choreographer for Ballets Russes.
- **Vaslav Nijinsky** → He was a star dancer with and controversial choreographer for Ballets Russes.
- **George Balanchine** → He is the "father of ballet in America" and the founder of the New York City Ballet.
- **Anna Pavlova, Rudolf Nureyev, and Mikhail Baryshnikov**→ These were Russian dancers who popularized ballet in America during the 1920s, 1960s and 1970s, and 1980s, respectively.

Contributing Individuals to Modern/Contemporary Dance

- **Loie Fuller and Isadora Duncan** → They were the progenitors of modern dance.
- **Ruth St. Denis** → She was the co-founder of Denishawn, the first modern dance school.
- **Ted Shawn** → He was the co-founder of Denishawn and the founder of Jacob's Pillow Dance Festival.
- **Doris Humphrey and Charles Weidman** → These Denishawn students produced the first modern dance performance and established the Humphrey (later Humphrey/ Limón) technique.
- **Martha Graham** → This Denishawn student, legendary dancer, and choreographer developed the Graham technique and established The Martha Graham Dance Company, the first dance company.
- **Lester Horton** → He established the Horton technique in Los Angeles and was a longtime partner of Bella Lewitzky.
- **Erick Hawkins** → He was a celebrated choreographer and the first male dancer for the Graham Company.
- **Merce Cunningham** → He was a legendary avant garde choreographer and the founder of the Merce Cunningham Dance Company.
- **Katherine Dunham, Pearl Primus, and Helen Tamiris** → They researched and injected African and Caribbean styles into modern dance.

- **Paul Taylor, Alvin Ailey, Jose Limón, and Alwin Nikolais** → They were notable later-generation choreographers.
- **Judson Church** → This was a post-modern dance collective established in the 1970s.

Contributing Individuals to Jazz Dance

- **Jack Cole** → This Denishawn dancer and Broadway choreographer invented "theater dance."
- **Katherine Dunham** → This Broadway and Hollywood performer and choreographer introduced African and Caribbean dance styles.
- **Jerome Robbins** → This Broadway and Hollywood choreographer choreographed the film version of "West Side Story."
- **Cholly Atkins** → This legendary tap dance partner of Charles "Honi" Coles also worked as a choreographer for artists with the Motown record label later in his career.
- **Ann Miller** → This Hollywood jazz and tap dancer popularized the practice of wearing pantyhose in place of stockings.
- **Bob Fosse** → This award-winning choreographer and musical director of "Cabaret," "Sweet Charity," and "All That Jazz" created the Fosse technique.
- **Gene Kelly** → He was a Broadway and Hollywood tap and jazz dancer, as well as a movie star.
- **Luigi** → He was a dancer with physical disabilities who created a therapeutic method that led to the development of standard jazz technique.
- **Gus Giordano** → This celebrated teacher founded the Jazz Dance World Congress.
- **Matt Mattox** → He was a celebrated teacher of jazz technique.
- **Twyla Tharp** → She was an award-winning choreographer of both Broadway and Hollywood jazz and modern dance.

Contributing Individuals to Tap Dance

- **Master Juba** → He was the first African American dancer to play to white audiences, and the only one to receive top billing in a white minstrel group.
- **Bill "Bojangles" Robinson** → He was a turn-of-the-century vaudeville hoofer who danced on Broadway and in Hollywood's Shirley Temple films.
- **Harold and Fayard Nicholas** → These brothers were famous in vaudeville, on the jazz circuit, and in Hollywood for their daring, acrobatic style.
- **Cholly Atkins and Charles "Honi" Coles**→ This duo became famous in the 1940s. Along with Cab Calloway, they were part of the big-band circuit, and they performed in Hollywood.
- **Ruby Keeler** → She was a Hollywood dancer who appeared in "42nd Street" and other films.
- **Fred Astaire and Ginger Rogers** → These Hollywood partners were famous for appearing in films that featured their supernaturally smooth ballroom and tap styles.
- **Sammy Davis, Jr.** → He was a Broadway, Hollywood, and Las Vegas dancer, singer, and actor.
- **Gregory Hines** → He was a Broadway/Hollywood hoofer and actor who ushered in the "tap revival" of the 1980s.
- **Savion Glover** → He is a new-generation Broadway/Hollywood tap and hip hop dancer and choreographer.

Josephine Baker, Katherine Dunham, and Beyoncé Knowles

Josephine Baker established herself as a dancer and singer during the Harlem Renaissance, and then quickly became a star in Paris. Her sensational performances often included elements of

African, Caribbean, and Asian cultures. These culminated in the iconic Danse Sauvage, in which she appeared wearing a skirt made of bananas. This spectacle is still imitated today.

An innovator in African American modern dance, Katherine Dunham integrated her classical ballet training with ethnographic studies of Caribbean dance forms and their African roots. While starring on Broadway and in Hollywood in the 1940s, she also established the country's only permanent, internationally acclaimed black dance troupe.

Beyoncé Knowles became the most highly acclaimed and highest paid female performer in the world in the 2000s. In keeping with the cultural sampling media tactics of the current era, her music videos often feature visuals and movements from other cultures. The Mozambican kwaito dance in her "Run the World" video is just one example.

Dance Across the Arts & Disciplines

Developing Dance Knowledge and Appreciation and Promoting Achievement

Nothing is more galvanizing, edifying, or informative for a novice than watching the work of a great performer, regardless of his or her chosen art form. Someone who is great at what they do helps others aspire to the same level of greatness, and motivates them to pay close attention to how it's done. Therefore, exposing students to great dance is one extremely effective strategy for developing dance appreciation and knowledge, and for promoting student achievement.

If possible, teachers can show students a video during every class meeting. Videos should feature accomplished dancers from various cultures, backgrounds, and historical periods performing different styles of dance. Though not every student will respond positively to every video, each will see something inspiring over time. Additionally, all students will gain exposure to the breadth and depth of greatness possible in the thousands of worlds that exist inside dance.

Developing Students' Observation and Evaluation Skills

Dance sometimes feels very different from the way it looks to an observer. Choreographing, performing, and analyzing dance require very different skills. The more students know about each, however, the more effective they will be at performing all three tasks. A good exercise will incorporate choreographing, performing, and analyzing. In one round, students break into groups of three. Student A choreographs a phrase and performs it for students B and C, who observe and give feedback on both choreography and movement. Then, students B and C learn the phrase. Each performs it for the other two, who observe and respond.

For the second round, this process is repeated with student B's choreography. For the third, it is repeated with student C's. At the end of the exercise, each student has created a work, interpreted it for both a choreographer and an audience, witnessed a performance, analyzed a performance, and communicated a critical response to both the dance itself and the dancer's performance.

Developing Analytical Powers of Observation, Reflection, and Evaluation

When teaching abstract skills through dance, the "theory plus practice" approach is often useful. This involves an initial discussion of the topic and the method intended to illustrate it, followed by student participation in the exercise, and then a discussion of the insights grasped as a result. For example:

- First, the teacher and the class discuss kinesthetic response (movement impulses that are involuntary reactions to watching movement) and the ways in which dance evokes thoughts, ideas, memories, and questions in observers.
- Second, the teacher divides the class into two groups. Group 1 is instructed to create some short movement combinations. Once they do this, Group 1 shows their movements to Group 2.
- Third, the groups switch places. Group 2 creates movements that are inspired by the kinesthetic response and emotional reactions to the movements performed by Group 1.
- Finally, both groups reflect and discuss thoughts that emerged and responses felt in the body while watching each other's movements. The process is repeated, except this time Group 2 shares their short movement combinations with Group 1, and Group 1 responds.

Improving Abilities to Observe, Reflect Upon, and Critically Evaluate Dance

Teachers can use discussions to introduce the idea of critical perspective. Discussions should highlight the critical focus on performance factors like technique, phrasing, energy, and impression, as well as on compositional concerns such as use of space and staging, timing, and sequencing of movements.

For younger students unfamiliar with critical analysis, role playing can be useful for introducing the process. Using humor and levity, placing an emphasis on constructive criticism, and switching roles so that everyone gets to act as both critic and performer can reduce the likelihood of sensitivity or shameful reactions. Older students will likely have been exposed to the process in the past, and may be somewhat proficient at critically evaluating dance.

After the idea of critical perspective has been introduced and discussed, students may work together and take turns performing and offering critiques, either as a group led by the teacher (for younger students) or one-on-one with occasional teacher input (for more advanced students).

Providing Students Opportunities to Analyzing Dances and Performances

Critical thinking is most effectively tested by asking a student to evaluate his or her own or another dancer's performance of a dance (whether performed as part of a classroom exercise or in a professional concert). Nothing clarifies thoughts more than being required to express them, either verbally or in writing.

After they are given ample exposure to technical requirements, movement quality concepts, assessment criteria, and constructive communication strategies, students are armed with the necessary knowledge to begin assessing their own and other's performances. This may be done verbally in a whole-class discussion (possibly employing Viewpoints or another system for analyzing and discussing dance), one-on-one, or in the form of a written assignment.

Choreography offers even more opportunities for analysis, as it involves so many elements, forces, and possibilities. First, becoming familiar with and manipulating choreographic elements requires comprehension, critical selection, and creative application. Second, analyzing the interaction of the forces at work in a finished dance requires perceptive discrimination and discernment.

Teaching Students Appropriate Behavior for an Audience Member

Teachers can use discussion in the classroom to inform students of the appropriate protocol for audience members at a dance performance. Then, if possible, taking a field trip to attend an actual performance would be ideal, as it would allow students to implement their knowledge. Teachers can advise students of the following guidelines for audience members:

Students should arrive well before show time, enter the theater and find a seat quietly, and turn off cell phones—and leave them off for the duration of the performance. Students should watch the entire performance quietly. There should be no talking, whispering, fidgeting, using phones, using flash photography, or eating candy with crinkly wrapping. Students should applaud at appropriate times. Once the show is finished, students should exit the theater calmly and, if they have a performer to congratulate, wait in the lobby.

Ideally, students will also pay attention to the impressions left on them by the dance's design, outstanding moments, and overall energy.

Encouraging Self-Expression and Dance to Respond to Their Environment

Creative movement experiences have been known to help students of all ages and backgrounds process information from other classes, as well as express thoughts and feelings about situations from both their own lives and the world at large.

The excitement and freedom of movement clears students' heads and allows them to process information more clearly. The exploratory, non-competitive environment of a public school dance class can be beneficial for all students, and has yielded especially effective results for at-risk students with ADHD or other behavioral issues and those with limited language capabilities.

In order to complement schoolwork, a teacher can develop exercises focusing on and illustrating principles from other classroom curricula, such as spatial concepts, geometric shapes, vocabulary and verbal expression, or cultural studies. To address personal situations or emotional issues, students can be encouraged to express their feelings—and to explore adjustments and resolutions—through movement.

Chapter Quiz

Ready to see how well you retained what you just read? Scan the QR code to go directly to the chapter quiz interface for this study guide. If you're using a computer, simply visit the online resources page at **mometrix.com/resources719/aepadance** and click the Chapter Quizzes link.

Dance Education

Kinesiology & Somatics for Dancers

Anatomy, Physiology, and Kinesiology

As artists, many dancers have a somewhat hostile attitude toward science. Since dance is a dynamic art form which requires a healthy, strong, flexible body as its instrument (and because almost no bodies are without inherent structural imperfections), familiarity with the sciences of body structure (anatomy), body functions (physiology), and bodies in motion (kinesiology) can be a great advantage to a dancer.

A theoretical understanding of proper skeletal alignment, muscle and joint action, and the action of gravitational forces upon the body can augment the kinesthetic perception that dancers cultivate daily within their bodies. This knowledge can further enhance the development of individually appropriate methods of physical conditioning and strategies for injury prevention. Such knowledge can also deepen a dancer's understanding of efficient motion and distinctive movement patterns, which can help the dancer improve performance and expression.

Kinesiological Terms Used to Describe Locations in the Body

- **Anterior** → Toward the front of the body, limb, or structure being described
- **Posterior** → Toward the back of the body, limb, or structure being described
- **Lateral** → Toward the side of the body, limb, or structure being described
- **Medial** → Toward the middle of the body, limb, or structure being described
- **Superior** → Toward the upper part of the body, limb, or structure being described
- **Inferior** → Toward the lower part of the body, limb, or structure being described
- **Proximal** → Closer to the center of the body, limb, or structure being described (most commonly used to describe limb structure)
- **Distal** → Farther away from the center of the body, limb, or structure being described (most commonly used to describe limb structure)

Kinesiological Terms Used to Describe Joint Action in the Body

- **Flexion** → The action of "bending" a joint, or the action of decreasing the angle between two levers
- **Extension** → The action of "straightening" a joint, or the action of increasing the angle between two levers
- **Hyperextension** → The action of "over-straightening" a joint past its natural angle, or the action of increasing the angle between two levers to more than 180 degrees
- **Abduction** → Movement of a limb away from the midline of the body (memory tip: abduction = taking away)
- **Adduction** → Movement of a limb toward the midline of the body (memory tip: think of "adding" to the body)
- **Rotation** → The action of "turning" a ball-and-socket joint; circular movement around a central axis
- **Inversion** → Inward rotation; turning a limb inward, toward the front of the body
- **Eversion** → Outward rotation; turning a limb outward, toward the back of the body

Human Skeletal Structure

The human body employs the strongest known structure—the arch—to stack the bones of the skeleton. This arch runs in two directions: longitudinally from toes to heel, and transversely from the inside to the outside edge of the foot. The arch forms a dome across the two feet when they are parallel to each other. While strong enough to support the body's weight and act as a foundation, the feet are equally capable of accommodating a wide range of motion due to the number of bones and joints they contain.

Foundation is also important because of its effect on the alignment of bones and joints built upon it. Proper alignment in the foot promotes proper alignment in all superior (higher) joints, enhancing precision of movement execution. Conversely, misalignment in the foot, which is exacerbated by gravity and force, can create a need for compensation. It can result in misalignment in the next closest joint and, if not addressed, all subsequent ones.

Systems of the Human Body That Most Affect a Dancer's Movement

The bones of the skeletal system form the framework that gives the body its structure, allowing it to resist gravity, remain in positions over time, and maintain balance. Joints within the skeleton allow for movement. The range of motion of each joint is determined by bone structure, ligament length and density, and muscular tension/flexibility. The skeleton affords only the potential for movement; the force required to produce motion is provided by the muscles.

The neuromuscular system initiates impulses in the brain, transmitting them via the nerves to the muscles, which contract and release to produce motion or to maintain a position in space. The tissue makeup, shape, and grouping of muscles vary according to where muscles are located and the functions they perform.

Connective tissues "knit together" the skeletal and muscular systems. Tendons connect bones to muscles, ligaments connect bones to bones, and fascia creates a flexible "net" around muscles, nerves, and blood vessels to provide support.

Kinesiological Analysis

Structural analysis involves studying the body's bones and ligaments. Key areas of focus are the shapes and positions of bones and ligaments relative to each other in joints, and the ways in which they allow or restrict movement in joints. This knowledge is instrumental in understanding and achieving proper joint and skeletal alignment, which plays an important role in preventing injury.

Neuromuscular analysis studies the muscles needed to produce action in a joint, including specific muscle types and larger muscle groups, and looks at the kind of contractions muscles must perform. This is essential for understanding which muscles can produce a specific action most efficiently, which can help reduce unnecessary muscular tension and wear and prevent injuries.

Biomechanical analysis focuses on the forces of physics involved in movement, the effect of gravity and other physical forces on the "levers" (long bones of the limbs and extremities) of the body, and the type and range of actions various forces can produce.

Movement Efficiency

Efficiency of movement can be defined as using only the required amount of muscular and energetic effort to perform an action. When a strong, flexible, well-aligned body performs a movement, a minimum amount of effort is exerted by the muscles for each movement. Afterwards, there is a minimum amount of tension remaining in the muscles.

Physically, movement efficiency means there is a proper proportion of mobility and stability in the musculoskeletal structures. Bones and joints are aligned well during movement, and muscles and connective tissues are working within their proper range of motion and endurance. Thus, efficient movement serves to not only conserve a dancer's energy, but also to prevent injury.

Artistically, efficient movement is unencumbered by extra effort, which is visible, or any accompanying (unintended and unnecessary) actions to compensate for structural problems. Movement that is clear and unencumbered by tension can best represent the choreographer's vision.

Proper Skeletal Alignment and Structural Integrity

Bones and joints that are optimally aligned safely respond to gravity and a dancer's body weight. During movement, a body in correct alignment transfers forces through the body and into the ground, without placing undue stress on joint structures. Dancers condition their bodies and minds to attain proper alignment, not only to achieve the most effective movements possible, but also to prevent injury.

Misalignment destabilizes a joint and makes it work inefficiently, creating stress. Extreme or prolonged and repeated stress on a joint can rupture cartilage or tendons, pull muscles, overstretch ligaments, and even deteriorate or calcify bones if they rub against muscles or other bones.

Misalignment in a joint can also create a chain reaction, as each surrounding joint is subjected to unbalanced forces due to the structural weaknesses of the first joint. The surrounding joints will then compensate for these unbalanced forces. If left unaddressed, misalignment in one joint could eventually lead to misalignment in all the body's joints.

Mobility and Stability

Mobility describes the ease of movement within a given joint. Mobility is determined by skeletal structure as well as musculature, but mainly by the length and density of ligaments that support the joint by joining bone to bone. People with loose ligaments are described as "hyper-mobile," and exhibit a greater range of motion. They are also more susceptible to joint misalignment.

Stability refers to a joint's ability to maintain a particular position over time. Stability helps preserve the structural integrity and alignment of individual joints, and enhances whole-body resistance to gravity in balances. People with shorter, denser ligaments tend to exhibit greater stability and a corresponding reduced range of motion.

An inverse relationship exists between stability and mobility. As mobility increases in a given joint or limb, stability decreases, and vice versa. Stability is associated with strength and maintaining alignment, and mobility with flexibility and range of motion.

Range of Motion

Range of motion describes the distance a joint can move from flexion to extension, as well as its direction of movement. Joints in the body vary widely in terms of their range of motion. Wrists and ankles can rotate almost 360 degrees, the knees can only flex posteriorly, and the sacroiliac joint barely flexes at all.

A joint's range of motion can be restricted by the shape and arrangement of its bones, the length and density of its ligaments, and the amount of tension or flexibility in the muscles surrounding it.

Traditionally, dancers strive for increased flexibility to achieve the greatest range of motion possible in all joints, which maximizes the number of shapes that can be formed with the body. However, pushing a joint past its intended range of motion can destabilize it and cause injury, and should be avoided.

Articulation as it Relates to Human Joints

Articulation is movement through the range of motion of a joint or a successive series of joints. An example is a "wave" movement made by the hand. The impulse begins in the wrist (carpals), moves through the palm (metacarpals), and travels through the fingers (phalanges).

- **Ball and Socket** → Possible movements: Flexion, extension, adduction, abduction, 360 degree rotation
  - Examples: Shoulder and hip
- **Hinge** → Possible movements: Flexion and extension in one direction
  - Examples: Knee and elbow
- **Pivot** → Possible movements: Rotation
  - Examples: Pronation or supination of the forearm, rotating the head
- **Gliding/Plane** → Possible movements: Assist with flexion/extension/rotation
  - Examples: Cuneiform ankle bones and carpal wrist bones (both are a series of tiny bones that glide across one another)
- **Saddle** → Possible movements: Flexion, extension, adduction, abduction, circumduction (but not axial rotation); these joints can perform simultaneous movements in more than one direction
  - Examples: Thumb and sternoclavicular joint
- **Condyloid** → Possible movements: Same as saddle joint
  - Examples: Jaw and the first joint of the index finger

Kinesiology Principles Can Aid Dancers

The first rule of every vocation is, "Know your equipment." To perfect their skills and technique, dancers rely heavily on how they feel inside and how they look in the mirror, but that internal and external knowledge can be greatly enhanced by theoretical and technical knowledge of their equipment and the tasks it needs to perform on a regular basis.

An awareness of alignment and the action of gravity on joints is necessary for almost every movement in dance, especially lifts and jumps, battements and kicks, weight-bearing movements, and inversions. Knowledge of joint actions and relative range of motion can be very useful when working on turnouts and extensions. It helps dancers learn what is natural, when to push to achieve a movement or position, and when to stop pushing. Familiarity with mobility and stability can help dancers tailor a conditioning plan to meet their own individual needs, as can an understanding of somatotypes and their individual requirements.

Cognitive Objectives of Kinesiology That Are Specifically Related to Dancers

The main **cognitive** objectives of kinesiology related to dancers and dancing are:

- Comprehension of basic human physiology as it relates to movement
- Understanding of human skeletal structure, its proper alignment, joint actions and restrictions, and individual differences in bone structure
- Familiarity with the human muscular system, the structural makeup of muscle tissue and how it relates to muscle function, muscular attachments and actions, mechanics of muscle contraction, and individual differences in muscular structure

- Knowledge of the force of gravity on a body and the range of muscular responses to gravity during movement and stillness, as well as practical applications of that knowledge
- Awareness of physical demands regularly placed on the dancer's body, and an understanding of ways to build physical potential and increase efficiency of motion in response to those demands
- Familiarity with and anticipation of common dance injuries, as well as methods of injury prevention and treatment

Practical Objectives of Kinesiology That Are Specifically Related to Dancers

The main **practical** objectives of kinesiology related to dancers and dancing are:

- Increasing a dancer's awareness and understanding of their own and others' movement capacities and limitations, and fostering comprehension and acceptance of how to capitalize on capacities as much as possible and address limitations
- Facilitating maximum growth and development in physical ability to achieve ever-increasing levels of technical and artistic excellence
- Fostering optimal muscular efficiency in as wide a range of movements as possible to use energy in the best possible way to avoid detrimental movement patterns and undue stress and injury, while still meeting the physical and artistic requirements for each movement
- Preventing injury through greater cognitive awareness of potential hazards and increased kinesthetic sensitivity to the messages sent by one's own body
- Recovering from injuries more quickly and completely by applying knowledge of beneficial rehabilitation practices
- Extending the practical length of a dancer's career through the achievement of the previous objectives

Somatotype System

The **ectomorph** has a lean body with enhanced flexibility due to a lack of muscular strength and loose connective tissues. The nervous system is efficient, leading to high neuromuscular tension. The circulatory and digestive systems are inefficient. The ectomorph exhibits exceptional range of motion and quickness in movement but lacks strength and endurance.

The **mesomorph** has a sturdy body with strong, dense musculature and connective tissues, resulting in good posture. With a normal digestive and endocrine system, the metabolism and energy levels are high, and the cardiovascular system is extremely efficient. These result in great strength and endurance, but a lack of flexibility.

The **endomorph** has a rounded body type. Functioning of the muscular and cardiovascular systems is adequate. The neurological system functions somewhat slowly. Capabilities for strength, endurance, and flexibility are normal, but the extreme inefficiency of the digestive system, low thyroid functioning, and low metabolism often result in excessive weight gain.

Somatic Practices That Address Need for Flexibility and Joint Mobility

- **Flexibility Training** → This refers to any system of stretching the muscles. It has a number of health benefits, including releasing muscular tension, correcting muscular imbalances, releasing lactic acid and toxins stored in muscles, maintaining natural muscle length and density, increasing the range of motion in joints, reducing pain, and enhancing physical performance.

- **Yoga** → Yoga is an ancient system of mental and spiritual centering combined with physical conditioning. It emphasizes coordinating the breath with movement, which creates organic and beneficial postures and movements. In addition to enhancing strength and stability, yoga can also foster relaxation of habitually tight muscles and connective tissues, resulting in greater joint mobility. Many forms of the practice feature elongating and widening stretches for the major and minor muscles of the torso, spine, limbs, extremities, neck, and head.

Pilates and Yoga

- **Pilates** → Pilates is a movement practice that focuses on building endurance, strength, and stability in the core muscles of the body (abdominals, hips, buttocks, spine, upper thighs, and shoulder girdle) through repeated exercises that induce muscular contraction and release. The numerous stretches that are part of Pilates also develop flexibility. Pilates can be done alone on a mat or on specially-designed resistance-training equipment that incorporates weights, springs, and pulleys. The method emphasizes concentration, precision, control, breathing, and flowing movements during practice.
- **Yoga** → Yoga is an ancient system of mental and spiritual centering combined with physical conditioning. Although many people think of yoga as "only stretching," the hatha, vinyasa, and other physical styles incorporate many extensions, balances, inversions, and holds that build muscular strength and stability in the pelvis, abdominals, spine, shoulder girdle, and limbs. Additionally, yoga emphasizes coordinating the breath with movement, which creates the most organic and beneficial postures.

Releasing Muscular Tension and Altering Detrimental Movement Behaviors

- **Feldenkrais** → This practice employs repetitive motions derived from fundamental gestures and natural movements to increase awareness of habitual movement patterns and release tension left over from old injuries and habits in order to expand range of motion in the joints.
- **Alexander Technique** → This focuses on recognizing habitual movement patterns and postures, as well as places of accumulated tension, and then altering patterns and postures to address associated problems. The Alexander Technique can help improve balance, muscular support and flexibility, coordination, and movement efficiency, resulting in increased energy and greater ease of movement.
- **Bartenieff Fundamentals** → Based on Laban Movement Analysis, this practice encourages a deepened awareness of the connections between mind, body, movement, and internal and external environments to enhance mobility and function.
- **Ideokinesis** → This employs mental visualization of carefully devised imagery with tactile input to enhance coordination of movement and adjust habitual posture and movement habits. The reasoning behind this practice is that if one can "see" efficient and aligned movement, one can achieve it.

Imagery to Stimulate a Dancer's Kinesthetic Awareness

Kinesthetic awareness is the ability to know where (and in what shape and condition) the body, limbs, and extremities are in space in any given position or movement. Dancers must be able to discern not only their speed, direction, orientation to vertical, balance, and relation to gravity, but also the state of their muscles (tension, length, contraction, etc.) and the position of their joints.

Input from teachers and choreographers is integral to developing a dancer's kinesthetic awareness, and imagery is an effective way to develop that sense. Often, teachers use sensory images to heighten perception of a particular body part or group of muscles. Examples include light rainfall on skin to help broaden the back and shoulders, a fist closing to help contract abdominal muscles, and a light shining onto (or out of) a chest that needs opening and lifting. Often, imagery can help establish a dancer's "muscle memory" for a certain movement.

Structural Integrity of a Dancer's Body

The fundamental goals related to the structural integrity of a dancer's body are an upright posture, appropriate alignment of joints, a strong abdominal core, spinal elongation upward from the pelvis, and flexible muscles that are relatively free of habitual tension.

Careful observation of a student's posture, energy, and movement patterns can reveal limitations or imbalances that may be addressed by conscientiously implementing various movement modalities.

In addition to regular warm-up and conditioning exercises, teachers can introduce small doses of various somatic techniques for enhancing joint alignment (Bartenieff Fundamentals), elongating the spine (Alexander Technique and yoga), balancing muscular use patterns (Ideokinesis), fortifying and integrating core support (Pilates method), releasing neuromuscular tension and improving kinesthetic awareness (Feldenkrais, Alexander Technique, and yoga), and expanding breath capacity (yoga).

Implementing one or more of these somatic practices will allow the dancer to achieve optimal strength, flexibility, coordination, and endurance.

Developing "Body Sense"

Teachers seek to help students develop an enhanced awareness of themselves, other dancers, and physical elements in relation to space.

Cultivating body sense in space involves developing kinesthetic awareness (a sense of the body's location, position, and orientation in space) and spatial perception (an awareness of the self, others, and objects in the environmental space, as well as an awareness of the spatial relationship and patterns between the self and other dancers). Exercises that require many students to share space and move through and around each other without colliding help develop body sense. Individual and group exercises conducted with closed eyes and/or in silence are especially helpful.

Along with cultivating body sense in space, students should also learn how to sense, identify, understand, and eventually use physical forces and phenomena (gravity, force, resistance, action and reaction, inertia, structural integrity, velocity, and momentum) that act upon their bodies while they perform and create dance. The application and illustration of these concepts during regular movement exercises can familiarize students with them.

Cultivating Movement Skills

- **Stability and muscle control** → The student maintains positions when static, contracts muscles, directs motion with clarity, maintains balance during and after motion, and ceases movement decisively. This skill can be strengthened with exercises that have quick starts and stops, holds, and balances.
- **Release and momentum** → The student releases muscle contractions fully, allows momentum in swings and falls, and returns to balance after moving off center. This skill can be developed by swings, falls, movements off center of gravity, and inversions.
- **Articulation** → The student sequentially "unfolds" or "folds" bones within a joint during flexion and extension, resulting in greater clarity and expressiveness of movement. Warm-up exercises in particular can concentrate on articulating different joints.

- **Axial and oppositional movement** → The student initiates movement from the core for expansive and integrated quality, and coordinates movement with the opposing limbs. This skill can be enhanced by stationary shape-making, "folding in" and "spreading out," and exercises that divide torso movement.
- **Locomotion** → The student covers ground and achieves amplitude when moving across the floor. Walking, running, and leaping exercises help clarify movements, and infuse them with quality, intention, and style.

Production Elements: Tech, Roles & Performance Quality

Dance Studios

Dance studios differ in their details, but all have certain elements in common. Some of them are outlined below.

Dance studios have one or more medium-to-large, open rooms that are used for classes and rehearsals. Rooms originally designed for dance will be entirely open with no obstacles, but remodeled spaces may have posts placed inconveniently near the center of the room.

Often, a wall in a dance studio features one or two wooden or fiberglass ballet barres, or there may be portable, freestanding barres. Another wall is usually covered by mirrors. Floors should be wooden, whether sprung or traditional, and may or may not be covered with marley vinyl. There is usually a sound system of some kind in one corner.

In addition to actual studio rooms, many dance studios feature some of the following: a reception area and/or waiting room for parents or incoming dancers, a dressing room with storage for bags and street clothes, and restrooms (which may or may not have showers).

Performance Venues

Performance venues can include small, medium, and large theaters, as well as sound stages, art galleries, nightclubs, warehouses, gymnasiums, homes, outdoor public spaces such as parks and courtyards, and just about any other place imaginable.

Most theaters include a lobby, an audience seating area, a booth for technicians, a stage on which the performance takes place, and a backstage area with dressing rooms for performers. Larger theaters can have an orchestra pit below or in front of the stage, tall flyspaces and catwalks above the stage, a scene shop and/or costume shop, and possibly storage space beneath or behind the stage.

The features of theater stages also vary, but share several common characteristics. There is a deep, wide floor that is open to the audience at the downstage edge (this location is sometimes demarcated by a proscenium and extended with an apron) and covered by a curtain or wall at the upstage edge. Curtains or "legs" are hung in the wings at either side to cover exits and entrances.

House Manager, Stage Manager, and Stagehands

The stage manager is the person in charge, and is responsible for ensuring all technical aspects of a production are executed properly. The stage manager knows the dance thoroughly; coordinates all schedules to arrange rehearsals and work sessions; ensures safety; facilitates communication between dancers, designers, and tech crews; communicates with the house manager during performances; and calls the cues to performers and sound, light, and video technicians during performances.

Stagehands prepare the performance space as needed. This might include loading equipment, constructing and moving scenery, hanging lights or speakers, manipulating props, or clearing and cleaning the stage and backstage areas.

The house manager looks after ticket reservations and sales (by telephone, in person, and online). The house manager also maintains the press and "comp" lists for free seating, distributes programs, and looks after accounting tasks such as collecting receipts (these might be for cash, check, credit card, or online transactions). The house and stage managers coordinate the start time of each show.

Dancer and Choreographer During Rehearsals and Productions

The choreographer begins the process by creating the dance and then teaching it to the dancer. The choreographer is also responsible for producing and communicating the rehearsal schedule, and for collaborating with the necessary professionals to produce the accompanying sound or music, lighting plot, and cues. The choreographer must also oversee the design and construction of costumes and any set or prop pieces for the dance. If the choreographer is also the artistic director, he or she must collaborate with music and sound designers, the stage manager, the facility technical manager, technicians, and the crew to ensure the production proceeds as planned in the performance venue.

The dancer's responsibility is to arrive on time for all necessary rehearsals, meetings, and performances. The dancer should have eaten, hydrated, slept, and conditioned himself or herself adequately to be able to fully focus on and efficiently perform movements and other required tasks. In the performance venue, dancers should follow all rules and instructions given to them, and should be respectful in their communications with all personnel.

Audience Member

The audience is a big part of the reason why dancers perform. Without an audience, dancers would simply dance in class, as there would be no reason to take to the stage. As such, dancers owe the audience much gratitude. However, audience members also have their own responsibilities to dancers during performances.

The ideal audience member arrives well before showtime, pays the ticket price with a smile, enters the theater quietly, chooses a seat promptly, and turns off his or her cell phone—and leaves it off. During the show, the audience member watches the entire performance quietly, and does not talk, whisper, fidget, use the phone, use flash photography, or unwrap food with crinkly wrapping. The audience member also applauds at appropriate times. Once the show is finished, the audience member exits the theater calmly. If the audience member has a performer to congratulate, he or she waits in the lobby or asks to be directed backstage.

Ideally, the audience member also pays attention to the impressions left on him or her by the dance's design, outstanding moments, and overall energy.

Sound and Lighting

Sound is an integral element in dance, deeply affecting the audience's experience during a performance. Music, sounds, and spoken words can be live or pre-recorded. In all except the tiniest of performance spaces, sound will usually need to be amplified during the performance so that both the audience and performers will be able to hear it.

Lighting not only makes the dance visible, but can also create a mood or environment, define or adorn a space, direct the audience's attention, establish performers' roles and relationships, and create special effects. Lights are hung above the stage or set at the foot or sides of the stage. During the performance, lights are directed onto strategic areas as the dance necessitates.

Each element (lighting and sound) is usually created, shaped, and overseen by its own designer. The lighting designer and sound designer both work with a crew to configure the correct technical setup, which is often executed during performances by a different technician.

Lighting Designer

All designers attend every necessary meeting and rehearsal, keeping their technical crews informed of necessary scheduling considerations.

The lighting designer assists the choreographer artistically and logistically in designing, engineering, and implementing an appropriate lighting plot. The lighting designer also coordinates with the technical manager of the production facility during production. Because lighting is a specialized craft, designers in this field have great creative freedom in shaping the design of the dance.

After becoming familiar with the dance, the lighting designer creates a lighting plot on paper, communicates it to the lighting/electrical crew, and oversees the hanging, wiring, placement, and focusing of instruments (lights). Once the general plot is in place, the lighting designer attends rehearsals to adjust the placement of lights based on the choreography and costumes. The lighting designer will also codify cues for changes in lighting. Once the final plot is agreed upon, the lighting designer creates a cue sheet and communicates it to the lighting techs working the board.

Sound Designer

All designers attend every necessary meeting and rehearsal, keeping their technical crews informed of necessary scheduling considerations.

The sound designer (who is often also the musical director) assists the choreographer in selecting, acquiring, formatting, and transmitting a dance's sound or musical accompaniment. Choreographers often work with music from the beginning of their process, and have definite requirements for accompaniment. Nonetheless, sound designers contribute a great deal of creative input.

Sound designers provide rehearsal music, secure usage rights, and handle sound equipment needs, coordinating with the facility technical manager during production. If there will be live music, the sound designer is also responsible for meeting musicians' needs. This may involve scheduling auditions and rehearsals, addressing union requirements, and procuring sheet music and equipment. If the music will be pre-recorded, the sound designer creates and oversees sound media (CDs/mp3s, etc.). The sound designer also creates music cue sheets, distributes music cue sheets to the sound tech crew, and oversees the crew during production.

Video Designer

All designers attend every necessary meeting and rehearsal, keeping their technical crews informed of necessary scheduling considerations.

The video designer assists the choreographer with all matters related to video projection used during a dance. In addition to providing creative input to support and develop the vision of the choreographer, the video designer has numerous logistical responsibilities: familiarizing himself or herself with the dance, procuring necessary video (whether it is from an existing source or new footage is needed), acquiring and formatting media, and compiling, processing, and editing footage into its final format.

The video designer also coordinates early on with the performance venue's technical manager to determine theater dimensions, projector locations, obstructions, video equipment needs, and other technical considerations. During production, the video designer attends rehearsals to coordinate video with lighting, sound, costumes, and choreography, and then designs a cue sheet and communicates it to all necessary personnel.

Costuming and Makeup

Costumes can enrich the overall impression a dance makes, and are chosen as carefully as any other design element. With their color, silhouette, fabric, adornment, and texture, costumes can suggest a time period or a mood, emphasize motion and speed, highlight space unoccupied by motion, draw attention to important body parts or particular performers, augment a defining movement quality, suggest groupings and relationships, and enhance the intensity of a dance. Even basic costumes acquired on a tight budget can permit freedom of movement, while communicating a sense of line, energy, focus, and tone.

Makeup used in dance is subjected to greater physical demands than that used in a regular theatrical setting. It is prone to running due to dancers' sweat (which may result in the makeup getting into and stinging the dancer's eyes), smearing during dancers' contact with each other and the floor, and changing color under the creative lighting choices that may be used in dance.

Costumer

The costumer attends all necessary meetings and rehearsals, familiarizing himself or herself with the dance and collaborating with the choreographer in order to design the costumes. Costume designers are usually granted a decent amount of artistic license in developing costumes. They typically expand upon the choreographer's ideas rather than simply execute them as presented. The task of costume design is often separate from costume construction. Because of its time-consuming nature, costume construction is almost always delegated to a crew of costuming assistants.

Ideally, costumers (or their crew) will take dancers' measurements; sew mockups for approval by the choreographer; schedule fittings; buy and prepare material and supplies; cut patterns; and sew, fit, alter, and repair costumes.

During the performance, the costumer (if part of the wardrobe crew) will transport the costumes and check them in and out. The costumer will also repair, launder, store, and safeguard the costumes between performances.

Prop Design and Construction

Sets and props are often less prevalent in dance than in traditional theater. This is because dancers mainly require open space and freedom of movement to perform. However, if used strategically, sets and props can add dimension and creativity to a dance.

Traditional theater sets are usually large, painted pieces of wood or fabric that simulate a particular setting or object. Sets in dance often play a different role: emphasizing specific design elements of a dance. Sometimes, set pieces are integrated into a dance, with dancers moving and climbing on them as part of the choreography. This requires extra consideration of safety and mobility issues during design and construction.

Generally, the use of props requires careful attention from a performer, and dancers often do not have the time or the means to handle and exhibit them while in motion. However, some dances are choreographed around a prop or a set of props to illustrate a central theme.

Props, Costumes, Makeup, and Hair

A dancer's performance can be affected by anything that comes into his or her personal space, which includes production elements such as props, costumes, makeup, and hair. These can all create distractions and/or discomfort. Dancers must prepare and compensate for these issues.

The proper handling of props, whether handheld or larger, requires extra attention and care. Most dancers would rather focus that extra attention on maintaining their technique, remembering choreography, and other important tasks.

Costume pieces that hang, catch, whip around, or fall off can cause not only annoyance, but also possibly dangerous distraction or movement obstruction for a dancer. Costumes that are too tight or too loose and ones that fit oddly can cause discomfort.

Heavy character makeup can run when a dancer sweats. Makeup can cause stinging if it gets into the eyes. False eyelashes obscure vision and result in a "hooded" sensation for the wearer. Wigs can slide off during strenuous movement, and especially heavy ones can alter a dancer's center of gravity.

Lighting Equipment

Since most studios do not have lighting options, lights rarely enter the equation until the lighting designer begins attending rehearsals. Once production begins, the technical considerations are many.

Instruments (or "cans") light the stage from above, from the foot, or from the sides. Lights are classified according to their function as floodlights or spotlights. Lighting types include PAR or parabolic, cyc/strip, Fresnel, and ERS or ellipsoidal, among others. Colored lighting can be achieved through the use of filters or "gels" attached to lights, and special effects can be achieved through the use of "gobos."

Lights are wired to dimmer packs, which allow power levels to be adjusted. They are connected through cables (or sometimes a wireless system) to the main light board. From this board, the lighting technician sets levels for each instrument and changes the settings for each cue. Modern light boards are often computerized, and one button can be used to record levels and change cues.

Sound Equipment

Sound designers or choreographers must address the technical needs of sound accompaniment during rehearsal and production. These needs can include formatting, playback, and amplification.

Because live accompaniment at every rehearsal is unheard of, rehearsal sound generally needs to be formatted onto a portable, distributable, repeatable medium, which could be a CD, mp3, or audio file. Studio playback can be done on a portable "boom box" stereo, a computer or mp3 player with plug-in speakers, or even a PA system.

During production, sound is almost always amplified by the performance venue's PA (public address) system, and is typically controlled by a sound technician at the sound board who sets volume levels and switches sound and music for each cue. Modern sound boards are computerized, and a single button can be used to record levels and change cues. Pre-recorded formats can make use of any of the technologies mentioned above, but live performances require amplifiers or direct inputs/pickups for instruments (usually provided by each musician) and microphones for vocals.

Video Equipment

Video for dance performances has its own unique set of technical considerations. First, room dimension has a large influence on the format and projection of video images, and must be considered during the initial editing and formatting of footage. Projector placement is another primary concern. If images are to be rear-projected, available backstage space and dimensions should also be considered. Screen and projector setup and placement should cooperate with and enhance, not interfere with, the lighting plot.

Since modern video production programs are computerized, an artist's software, files, media, and computer equipment must be compatible with the venue's computer operating system, projector(s), cables, and control board. Types of equipment can vary immensely from venue to venue. Often, video projection is controlled through the artist's computer rather than the venue's centralized board, which is used to control traditional sound and lighting.

Rehearsals

After the relatively lengthy period of studio rehearsals, in which dancers learn and perfect choreography, production begins. At this point, the rehearsals move to the performance venue. These vary widely according to their purpose and the design elements that will be incorporated into the rehearsal.

Spacing rehearsals allow the dancers to become accustomed to the dimensions and particular features of the performance space. They may also be useful for lighting designers, as they can help designers figure out how to focus the lights onstage.

Cue-to-cue rehearsals are held for the benefit of the stage and technical crews. They allow crew members to familiarize themselves with technical cues. These often do not involve any performance of movement, but require dancers to "stand in" at each spot where cues for music, lights, video, or stage direction change.

Dress rehearsals combine all of a show's production elements—costumes, sound, lighting, video, sets, props—into a run-through that looks as much like the actual performance as possible. These usually happen immediately before a performance.

Logistical Factors

A clean performance space, admission and seating processes that are ordered and show attention to detail, legible programs, a thoughtful opening address, and quick, smooth transitions between pieces are all characteristics of a production executed by an organized and professional cast and crew.

Lighting has a subtle yet powerful effect on an audience. Aside from the lighting requirements for each individual dance, there are other lighting considerations. House lighting should be bright enough to allow audience members to read programs, but soft enough to create a pleasant atmosphere. Stage lights should be carefully focused to avoid shining them into audience members' eyes from any possible sightlines.

Staging can be tailored for all audience sizes and types of spaces. A deep stage or apron allows dancers to work far downstage to avoid the impression of "dancing in a hole." A small, intimate space requires careful staging that makes the most of the proximity of audience members without "dancing in their laps."

Sequence and Presentation of Programming

A show that is too short (less than half an hour)—unless admission is free—can make audience members feel like they "haven't gotten their money's worth." However, most shows are too long (over an hour and a half with intermission), leaving audience members feeling fatigued and irritated by the end.

In a mixed program, variety is practically built into the programming. This is an advantage, as not everybody likes every kind of dance, and greater variety offers more opportunities for audiences to connect with a piece. However, if the program features the work of just one choreographer, audiences expect a more cohesive show.

The sequencing of a performance program, similar to a narrative or a dance, has an energetic flow that can be adjusted to have the greatest possible impact on the audience. Generally, the aim is to grab attention with the first piece; follow with slower, lighter pieces that increase in energy; and then finish with the strongest, most energetic work.

Sequencing and Presentation

Whether within the confines of a single dance or across the whole breadth of a concert, variety and contrast will keep audiences interested and anticipating "what's coming next." This does not require sensationalism, but a careful eye to identify excessive repetition or uniformity of elements. Dances must contain sufficient vocabulary to keep the work from "saying the same thing" repeatedly. Dances that are very similar in terms of their visual elements, accompaniment, or energy should be separated in the program.

Pacing choices also affect an audience's experience immensely. Within a single dance, movements must be sequenced in a way that varies the dance's energy over time, giving it an overall sense of transformation. The same should be done for dance pieces across an entire concert. Skillfully sequencing the energy and type of dances in a program can lead audiences on an energetic journey, enhancing their impression of variety and excitement.

Appropriate Behavior While Performing in a Dance Event

Teachers can use discussion in the classroom to initially prepare students to meet the particular behavioral expectations for dancers in a performance setting. Then, if possible, taking a field trip to tour a theater would be beneficial, as it would allow the teacher to walk students through all areas that are important to performers. Ideally, the teacher would suggest proper protocol for each area, and would provide a basic timeline of events for rehearsals and performances in the venue.

In this setting, teachers can emphasize the need for dancers to pay attention to backstage hazards, sightlines from offstage and behind curtains, the authority of the stage manager, and the duties and needs of the technical crew.

Teachers should also clearly state general expectations for dancers, including punctuality, physical and mental readiness (including a preparedness for long waits and/or hurried interactions in uncomfortable conditions), and alertness. Dancers are also expected to be considerate towards all other parties during the rehearsal and production process.

Projection, Confidence, Expression, Rhythmic Sense, and Musicality

Classroom experiences should consistently stress the importance of performance qualities to foster an awareness of their importance in students. Teachers can discuss with students the different necessities and opportunities related to dancing in a classroom and onstage, and can remind students to practice emitting performance level energy.

To elicit projection, expression, and confidence from students, enthusiastic verbal cues are essential. Suggestions along the lines of "playing to the back row," "letting them see your face," and "claiming your spotlight" can be helpful. To develop rhythmic sense and musicality in students, they should be encouraged to listen attentively to the music. This may even involve stopping and repeating sections to emphasize a particular rhythmic feature.

Finally, nothing galvanizes a dancer's movements more than actually performing in front of an audience. Opportunities for students to perform in front of friends and family in a setting that is as authentic as possible will familiarize them with the nervousness, excitement, and particular requirements of performance.

Performance Qualities That Make Dance Expressive, Dynamic, and Interesting

Dance teachers can use encouragement, imagery, and examples to introduce and develop performance qualities in students.

Praise and positive reinforcement heighten the quality of a student's performance. When students know they are being watched, appraised, and judged as successful, they not only internalize the feeling of success, but also hunger for more, "playing to the audience" with greater animation and confidence.

During movement exercises, a teacher's verbal cues employing imagery can be especially useful for alerting students to qualities such as facial and movement expressiveness, projection, confidence, rhythmic sense, phrasing, and musicality.

Also useful are videos featuring the work of professionals whose styles exemplify particular elements of performance quality—the dynamism of Paula Abdul, the effortless delicacy of Maria Tallchief, the rhythmic sense of Gregory Hines, etc. The combination of visual examples and artistic role models can be especially persuasive for teenagers, who are often searching for mentors, and are especially attuned to success in popular culture.

Personal Factors

Providing adequate time for rehearsal is largely up to the choreographer, who schedules rehearsals. However, it is the dancer's responsibility to request extra rehearsals if he or she feels underprepared for an upcoming production.

Technical skill is a function of innate talent, physical conditioning, and technical training. Innate talent is the luck of the draw, but dancers can take control over conditioning their bodies to minimize limitations and maximize capacities. They can also constantly train to improve their dance technique.

A dancer's energy—both the physical reserves they call upon during exertion and the particular quality of attitude and effort they put into movement—is affected by basic factors such as adequate sleep, nutrition, hydration, and stress release.

Focus (a dancer's will and ability to fully concentrate physically and mentally on every moment of a dance) and expression (the ability to communicate emotional states through gesture and facial expression) are intangible qualities that are readily visible to audiences.

Evaluating Relative Success

Dancers are the vehicles that bring the choreographer's vision to the audience, so much of the success of a dance naturally depends on their performance. The most fundamental requirement of a successful dance is that dancers must possess sufficient technique and training to perform the movements as the choreographer intended. Dancers must have also had enough rehearsal time to become familiar and comfortable with movements, not only their basic form, but also the finer nuances of timing, pacing, and energy.

Ideally, transitions between movements appear smooth, and entrances and exits appear organized. Dancers avoid collisions with set pieces, lights, and other dancers in ensemble pieces. All interactions between dancers onstage, in fact, appear comfortable and deliberate, whether they are exchanging gestures from across an entire stage or coming into close contact to perform the loftiest lifts or tightest rolls.

The production elements of sound, lighting, costuming, and makeup (as well as set pieces, props, and video, if they are used) should all enhance the effect of a dance's movements. They should help achieve the choreographer's desired effect.

Sound accompaniment is a major element that works with movement, providing strong cues to the audience about the energy and intentions of the piece. Ultimately, it will reflect the dance's scope (from huge ensemble to solo), context (silence for serious subjects, novelty songs for comedy, etc.), and its aesthetic and energetic qualities.

Lighting establishes the mood of the dance, and its color, intensity, and direction will complement movement. It should not upstage, overpower, or confuse movements, but enhance them.

Appropriate makeup will correspond with the size of the venue (too much in a small venue is clown-like, while too little "disappears" on the face), the tone of the piece, and the character of each dancer.

Additional Art Forms in the Production of Dance Performances

Anyone who currently attends dance performances has most likely noticed the steady integration of non-dance art forms into dance. Projections of film footage and computer graphics have become standard elements in some choreographers' work, and interaction between dancers onstage and dancers onscreen is now common.

Spoken word—whether pre-recorded or live, whether the delivery is simple and straightforward or presented in the rhythmic format of "slam poetry"—is also increasingly used in place of (or in addition to) musical accompaniment.

This trend is the result of several forces, but is mostly related to the widespread availability of technology. More people than ever before are becoming proficient in burgeoning art forms such as graphic design, computer animation, film editing, sound editing and design, etc. Social networking puts more artists in touch with each other, facilitating cross pollination between art forms. All of this serves to answer the global audience's call for entertainment with more moving parts.

Among Dance, Mime (Pantomime), and Theater

Dance, mime, and theater are dynamic, expressive arts. Their common goal is to express ideas and feelings through action. Each form has borrowed specific skills from the others to further develop its own capabilities.

Pantomime and dance are both essentially wordless forms of communication. Mime's vocabulary is limited to gestures and facial expressions, whereas dance vocabulary can be more abstract and varied. The two have been intertwined throughout history, with mime used to promote enhanced understanding of many Romantic and Classical-period ballets.

Although staging and expressive concerns can be quite different for actors and dancers, theater and dance still share many of the same logistical concerns when performed onstage. These include completing entrances, exits, and transitions; responding to cues; hitting the correct mark on the stage plot; and adequately projecting the performers' energy into the audience. Dance has adopted many theatrical production elements, such as lighting, makeup, set design, and props.

Curriculum Design & Instructional Planning in Dance

Similarities in Form and Expression Between Dance and Other Art Forms

As art forms, dance and music enjoy an unusually tight affinity. The two intersect mainly in their use of time, force, and energy. Each manipulates the elements of beat, tempo, rhythm, meter, syncopation, and sequence (through the form of canon, for example) to create a particular mood or feeling. Force and energy are varied in phrasing and dynamics in both forms. Additionally, improvisation is featured as a means of creative, spontaneous expression in certain styles of each art form.

Although dance is a dynamic (moving) art form and visual arts are mainly static (excepting kinetic sculptures and some other types), the two areas overlap in their use of space and design elements. Shape, form, dimension, plane, and other fundamental concepts of visual art also serve as basic elements in the development of choreography. Both forms also explore the pull between spatial tension and visual balance, negative and positive space, asymmetry and symmetry, and curves and straight lines.

Relationship with Other Studies

Relationship Between Dance, Social Studies, and Language Arts

The main objective of dance is to express thoughts and ideas—this is also the main objective of language. Dance could be considered just another language, akin to ASL (American Sign Language), semaphore (the flag-positioning signals used by military and industrial workers), or other movement-based forms of communication. When comparing language and dance, words can be compared to movements. Phrases are obviously phrases, and dances can be viewed as entire essays or novels. Just as different countries and cultures have identifiably different languages, the dances of different cultures also have different attributes.

Dance is a primary communicator of culture, illustrating a community's landscape, livelihoods, social standards, spiritual priorities, and history through movement. As such, it can be identified as a natural area of interest in social studies. Indeed, many anthropological studies include native dances among the basic attributes of a people's culture.

Relationship Between Dance, Math, and Science

Often, artistic disciplines are regarded as the exact opposite of scientific or mathematic ones. However, dance, math, and science share a fundamental common denominator: the quest to understand and navigate the physical world by organizing it into different systems.

Physics and kinesiology are an example of the intersection between dance and science in that they both study the effects of physical forces on structures of the human body during movement. Gravity, force, resistance, action and reaction, inertia, structural integrity, velocity, momentum, and other scientific concepts not only act upon the body during dance, but also frequently end up as subjects of choreography because of the interesting visual images they inspire.

Math and dance often intersect in terms of their geometric and temporal studies. This is most easily seen in the choreographic design elements of shape, grouping of dancers, and arrangement and sequencing. The latter is especially visible in canon, and in the relationship between music—an inherently mathematical form—and dance.

Relationships Between Dance and Design or Architecture

Dance and design or architecture are connected most essentially through their mutual focus on the use of space. This results in a cause-and-effect relationship that works in both directions:

- **Design of the human body**: First, the human body is a structure in itself, designed and "built" according to the same principles as buildings and other edifices. It is also affected by the same forces of physics, time, gravity and weight, foundation, and use and wear. Bodies are made of bones, muscles, tendons, ligaments, fascia, nerves, organs, soft tissues, and liquids instead of wood, steel, and concrete, but the structural principles are much the same, a fact revealed through the study of anatomy.
- **Design as used by the human body**: Dance relies on design elements as the "building blocks" of choreography, working with the concepts and variations of shape, form, symmetry and asymmetry, curves and straight lines, dimension, spatial tension, and negative and positive space to create the shapes and images of a dance.

Skills That the Pursuit of Dance Can Instill and Foster

Obviously, daily dance training can shape a dancer's body into a strong, flexible, coordinated machine, and years of physicality offer a deep understanding of the human body. The study of dance can also cultivate many other valuable mental and emotional attributes.

Because dance is a demanding field of study both physically and mentally, and because it is not traditionally well-supported by educational or industrial institutions, dancers gain attributes related to mental "toughness," such as self-reliance and self-discipline. They "do it for the love of the dance."

Dance also promotes skills related to mental agility, such as memorization and the ability to shift movements or sequences in space and time. Making choices among endless improvisation or choreographic options hones creative problem solving skills. Ensemble work (especially contact) cultivates open-minded cooperation, communication, and collaborative skills.

Additionally, the particular demands of dancers' daily schedules tend to make them highly organized and efficient.

Skills and Abilities Cultivated Through the Study of Dance

The mental acuity and organization that dancers learn through the daily practice of envisioning, realizing, and adjusting design in space and time; their ingrained understanding of the human body as a structure in motion; and their constant management of demanding scheduling can be immensely helpful in carrying out the exacting theoretical and applied practical work required in both mathematics and science.

Mutual communication and creative cooperation skills, which dancers acquire through completing ensemble work and collaborating with other creative professionals and technicians, can be highly beneficial in social studies. In particular, the open-minded inquiry that dancers cultivate can be useful when working with unfamiliar populations and subcultures.

Since dance is essentially a form of communication, it has a natural affinity with language arts. Dancers regularly strive to achieve greater articulation and more effective expression, as well as a deeper understanding of communication directed towards them.

Mental and Emotional Skills Acquired

Organization and mental agility are valuable assets in almost any career, including engineering, architecture, construction, finance, information technology, transportation, and all forms of administration.

Self-discipline can be especially useful in any occupation that requires repetition or constant trial and error, such as scientific research, service industry work, writing (text or computer code), agriculture, and freelance work of any kind, as it is largely self-directed.

The creative problem solving abilities cultivated in dancers are useful in many fields, such as nonprofit administration, sales, social services, event production, law, media, and every kind of artisan work.

Many dancers capitalize on their superior familiarity with the human body and easy connection with other people by establishing a second career in healing arts or medicine. Others transfer their specific body of knowledge to the next generation by entering the field of education (which also requires all of the above attributes).

Instruction That Integrates an Understanding of Dance and Other Art Forms

Exercises in which students physically interpret other art forms are especially effective at emphasizing commonalities. Teachers can instruct students to "dance other arts" in these ways:

- **Visual art** → Teachers can guide students in exploring space, shape (curves and lines, spirals, angles, etc.), and light. Students represent the shapes and lines of a visual pattern through dance, motionlessness, and locomotion.
- **Architecture** → Teachers can instruct students to explore the effect of space on movement (ducking under imagined low ceilings, dodging pillars, etc.) or illustrate architectural shapes. For the latter, a group of students can be told to lie down, sit, or stand to create a "building" with their bodies.
- **Music** → This type of instruction can involve exploring spatial relationships (spaces between notes as spaces between movements or dancing bodies), similarities in time (movements with different tempos, sequencing, beginnings, durations, and endings), or physical representations of pitch and texture (movements that "look like" vibrato, crescendo, etc.).

- **Writing** → This type of instruction can involve exploring parallels between communicative units, as well as equating sounds with movement impulses, words with movements, phrases with phrases, sentences with movement sequences, and paragraphs with entire combinations.

Instruction That Integrates an Understanding of Dance and Other Disciplines

Exercises in which students physically interpret concepts from other disciplines are effective at revealing their relevance to and interactions with dance. Teachers can instruct students to create and perform short phrases exploring these concepts by using the following approaches:

- **Math** → Exercises may involve examining geometric shapes, spatial paths, floor patterns, or spatial arrangements of dancers; adding or subtracting the number of bodies dancing or the units of space covered by movement; multiplying time increments through canon; and adding through repetition.
- **Science** → The forces of physics and how they affect bodies in motion can be explored through exercises that emphasize gravity, balance, speed, force, buoyancy, and pressure. Exercises may also involve mimicking the movements of cell components.
- **Social studies** → The concept of culture can be explored by having students "dance about" aspects of their daily lives. Exercises may also involve asking students to illustrate everyday movements or represent dreams, aspirations, and past experiences through dance.
- **Language arts** → Storytelling, character, and timeframe can be represented through gesture, expression, shape, and spatial choices in movement.

Goals of Response and Evaluation

The response and evaluation component focuses on numerous aspects of dance's function and value in society—when it's good, what it's good for, who thinks so, what it compares to, how it's valuable, etc. Becoming knowledgeable about the essential elements, implications, expectations, and etiquette of the world of dance, as well as its various cultural contexts around the world develops critical and creative thinking as well as decision making and communication skills.

This curriculum seeks to expand the student's knowledge of dance's cultural context and significance in art forms (such as music, theater, and visual art), different disciplines (such as math, science, social studies, and language arts), and society at large. Students also learn to analyze a variety of dance forms from several perspectives (dancer, choreographer, critic, or audience member) and recognize the value of dance-related skills in workplace experiences.

National Standards in Dance

These standards guide assessment throughout elementary, middle, and high school, and establish competencies for content and achievement for students in grades 4, 8, and 12. These seven main areas of student assessment include:

- Identifying and demonstrating movement elements and skills in performing dance (learning and performing technique for different forms)
- Understanding choreographic principles, processes, and structures (creating dance through choreography)
- Understanding dance as a way to create and communicate meaning (assimilating dance as an expressive art form)
- Applying and demonstrating critical and creative thinking skills in dance (dance-related mental and emotional skills)

- Demonstrating and understanding dance from various cultures and historical periods (knowledge and context of global dance)
- Making connections between dance and healthful living (applying principles of nutrition, hydration, rest, tension/relaxation, and conditioning)
- Making connections between dance and other disciplines (placing dance in a larger world context)

Cross Disciplinary Categories of Dance Knowledge and Proficiency

- **Supportive knowledge** → This includes a knowledge of how to define individual dance forms; a familiarity with dance vocabulary, history, and culture; and adherence to rules related to proper etiquette and attire.
- **Physiological training and conditioning** → This includes a knowledge and application of components of fitness, such as principles of exercise, types of activity, training factors, nutrition, weight control, etc.
- **Technique and choreography** → This includes comprehension and implementation of dance vocabulary, an ability to choose and work with appropriate music or other sound accompaniment, and the development of both teacher-created and student-created choreography.
- **Psychosocial development** → This includes compliance with classroom conduct rules and expectations; personal development in communication with the self, the teacher, and others; and development of group collaboration skills.
- **Artistic development** → This includes an understanding of aesthetic principles, the artistic demands of each dance form as well as its production and performance; and attributes of the dancer who is striving to develop artistry.

Assessment Strategies in Dance Education

Assessing Students' Progress

Assessment in dance is necessary, and allows both the student and the teacher to determine the following:

- The objectives of the class: knowledge to be gained, skills to be developed or mastered, and processes to be experienced
- Expectations of student behavior and achievement within the class environment
- Whether, how quickly, and how effectively the student is learning, assimilating, and retaining class material
- The student's strengths and limitations from one class meeting to the next, and his or her overall progression
- Any areas of the student's performance in class that require special attention to correct or enhance

The progress of dance students is generally assessed in three areas:

- **Dancing**: Includes skills involved in the development of technique as well as performance
- **Making dances**: Understanding and implementing the elements and processes of choreography to make dance
- **Analyzing dances**: Includes skills used to understand and critically analyze dances and performances

Technique is assessed for proper form, skill in executing movement, adherence to the rules of particular dance forms, and comprehension and application of movement principles. Performance can be evaluated on correct performance of movements and sequences, rhythmic competency, movement quality, and expression. (Additional criteria may include attitude, etiquette, and professionalism.)

Choreography is evaluated according to whether there is evidence of a student's understanding and creative use of the choreographic elements of space and design, time and rhythm, energy and force, relationships, choreographic devices, and compositional structures in the creation of dance. Knowledge of production and presentation may also be assessed.

Critical analysis is assessed based on evidence of a student's ability to understand and analyze dance through the various elements of form, genre, choreographic intention, environmental factors of presentation and production elements, and cultural and historical context. Verbal and written communication of such analysis is often assessed under this category, as well.

Models for Dance Curriculum and Assessment

- **Process model** → The student's creative growth is assessed in terms of levels of fluency, frequency, originality, and imagination in finding unique ways to solve movement problems. It is used in creative movement, improvisation, and choreography. Assessment forms include process folios, portfolios, and group projects.
- **Product** (or performance) **model** → This emphasizes the acquisition of ever-higher levels of technical skills. It is the standard model used in technique classes. Assessment forms include performance testing, rating scales, and written testing.
- **Combination model** → This combines the best of the process and product models, and focuses on three aspects: artistic (involving technique and performance), aesthetic (emphasizing perception, observation, and evaluation of performances), and cultural (examining dances' geographical, social, and political contexts). Forms of assessment include rubrics and contracts.
- **Discipline-based model** → This combines content and skills in dance history, criticism, aesthetics, and production/ performance, beginning with fundamental skills in elementary school, and gradually adding more complex and abstract skills as the student matures and progresses.

Assessing the Different Abilities and Experience Levels of Individual Students

Assessing individual students' technical development in dance can be done by considering the following elements:

- **Knowledge** → Understanding specific movements, sequences, and transitions in between
- **Timing** → Matching the correct movements with their intended counts, and implementing proper phrasing
- **Execution** → Performing each movement using the correct technique
- **Placement** → Using correct alignment of joints and other body principles throughout movement
- **Energy** → Employing appropriate energy and movement quality for each movement
- **Musicality** → Informing movement with an awareness of music, breath, and phrasing

Students may be evaluated on the basis of how often they fulfill each of the criteria on a checklist (checked the corresponding number of times) or a rating scale during a given testing exercise, combination, or class session.

Another method is to use a rubric to evaluate whether the student correctly performs one of the criteria rarely, sometimes, most of the time, or always. Other descriptions may also be used.

MOTOR LEARNING

In the verbal-cognitive stage of motor learning, a student mentally focuses on consciously understanding how to perform a task. The learner's concentration is on the technical aspects of distinct movements. Instruction often includes demonstrations and verbal explanations or cues to develop the basic movement pattern. This is a very conscious stage as the student is just beginning to understand the "vocabulary" of the movement. While the name may sound like language is tied up in this stage, and while verbal cues are helpful, this stage is not directly tied to language.

The motor stage is associated with a deeper focus on the specific mechanics of particular movements. The teacher detects errors and addresses them through prescriptive feedback and the repetition of specific approaches to problematic movements. Teachers can employ greater imagery and repetition here, introducing variations in and relationships between movements.

At the autonomous stage, a student's kinesthetic sense and motor memory are sufficiently developed to perform phrases and combinations without thinking about individual components. The student can now "dance" the movements. This allows for the development of mental skills such as mental review, imagery, and focus, as well as psychological skills such as a positive attitude, confidence, and self-counseling.

INSTRUCTIONAL STRATEGIES FOR SPECIAL NEEDS STUDENTS

All students respond to positive reinforcement. In technique classes, there should be an emphasis on the importance of basics. In ballet, for instance, prima ballerinas concentrate on basic pliés and tendus alongside novices.

On the other hand, more advanced students should be encouraged to progress, even as less advanced students maintain focus on basic elements. This requires keen observation of each student's capabilities and limitations. It also requires careful curriculum planning, which includes developing realistic movement modifications for students with special needs.

When teaching technique, simple exercises can have varying levels of difficulty. Opportunities to practice more difficult movement combinations (by adding double turns, incorporating extra beats, or inserting movements, for instance) should be incorporated when possible.

Teachers must also take into account students' learning styles. Classes usually contain a mix of kinesthetic, visual, and auditory learners, so integrating all kinds of sensory input (adding visual representations as well as audible and tactile cues and adjustments) is important.

EVALUATION FORMATS FOR ASSESSING STUDENT PROGRESS IN MOVEMENT SKILLS

- **Performance tests** → The teacher defines criteria and creates movement combinations requiring those particular skills. The student learns, practices, and performs the combinations while the teacher videotapes the performance. The teacher then uses the recording to evaluate the performance with a checklist or rating scale.
- **Checklists** → Criteria are established for the requirements of performing each movement. The student either does (check) or does not (no check) fulfill the requirements.
- **Rating scales** → The teacher creates a numeric scale, designates criteria for the highest and lowest levels, and rates each student's performance on the scale. A prominent example is the Likert scale, which uses a 4- or 5-point scale for ranking student performance.

- **Rubrics** → The teacher establishes criteria to be measured, describes individual skills related to each category, establishes a ranking system (usually 3 or 4 levels), creates indicators and descriptions for all performance levels, and then assesses student performance using the criteria being measured.

Evaluating Student Progress in Written and Verbal Communication

- **Written tests** → These are examinations used to assess knowledge gained. They can include true/false, matching, short-answer completion, multiple choice, or essay questions. They can be scored using points on a grading scale or percentages. They may also be graded on a pass/fail basis.
- **Contracts** → The student identifies his or her present level of ability, skills he or she needs to work on mastering, and the level of achievement desired. The student later performs a self-analysis and consults with the teacher to assess his or her progress.
- **Journal** → This is a student's collection of personal reflections on dance exercises, daily self-assessments and goals, feelings toward the class, assignments such as dance analyses, and choreographic processes.
- **Process folio** → This is a student's record of insights gained through the learning process. It focuses on production, reflection, perception, and approach.
- **Portfolio** → This is a chronologically ordered collection of all works pertaining to a student's learning experience (written assignments, videos, photographs, journals, self-evaluations and ones done by the teacher, etc.).
- **Oral reports** → These involve the verbal delivery of assignments such as dance concert reports, video reports, etc.

Formative, or Continual, Assessments of Dance Knowledge and Skills

Formative evaluation is the kind of ongoing assessment that takes place daily (or at every class meeting) as a result of the teacher's constant attention to students' continuing evolution.

The teacher assesses students as they perform in class, "bookmarking" for later examination the areas that individual students need to work on, as well as areas in which students are progressing or nearing mastery. After each class session, the teacher makes notes about the content of the lesson and the aforementioned observations of specific students' progress.

These insights may be shared immediately, but are usually stored away for use in particular situations in which insights about a student's technique would be useful to share. When planning lessons, this accumulated knowledge of each student's progress can serve as the basis for subsequent lessons that are compatible with general levels of student readiness.

Conducting Summative Assessments of Dance Knowledge and Skills

Summative assessment is the kind of formal evaluation that happens at intervals during and at the end of the semester (or other period). It allows teachers to arrive at an overall value of each student's cumulative work. This type of assessment can take the form of performance tests, written assignments, oral presentations, group projects, or full performances.

Formal evaluations of any kind should include conversations between the teacher and student afterward to discuss results and subsequent plans for improvement. They should also be scheduled with adequate intervals in between to allow students to progress between evaluations. Students should be given plenty of notice so they have time to prepare.

To best track a student's progress during a given time period, periodic, formal summative assessments should be combined with ongoing, formative assessments.

Review Video: Formative and Summative Assessments
Visit mometrix.com/academy and enter code: 804991

Methods of Self-Evaluation to Improve Technique

The inclusive style of teaching offers students the opportunity to self-evaluate by introducing movement combinations with different levels of difficulty. Teachers offer options to make the movement more challenging, such as adding more steps, accelerating speed, or changing direction during a combination. Each student can then choose an option based on their evaluation of how much difficulty they can handle. This can be an especially eye-opening self-evaluation for students, allowing them to truly understand their actual level of proficiency.

In the self-check style of teaching, the teacher either gives cues or develops (in conjunction with the student or alone) a checklist for the execution of a movement or combination. The student performs the movement or combination, observes himself or herself in the mirror (or on videotape in certain circumstances), and evaluates the execution using the criteria provided. In this way, the student takes responsibility for both teaching and learning the movement.

Several teaching styles allow students to observe, evaluate, and correct themselves when practicing technique, but not all are appropriate for beginning students. Guided discovery is an easy method teachers can use to introduce all but the youngest students to the habits of self-evaluation and self-correction (and convergent thinking or finding the "right" answer). This method can be used for more advanced studies of improvisation and choreography, as well.

The teacher asks a yes-or-no question designed to draw attention to placement or technique, such as, "Are your knees pointing out over your toes in demi plié?" Students observe themselves in the mirror or in person (looking down or at the specified body part) to discover the answer. Once the answer is clear (and if the answer is no), almost all students will automatically adjust their positioning or performance accordingly. Student participation also offers the benefit of retention for future reference.

Constructive Feedback

Teachers should offer positive feedback to students as often as possible to reinforce positive techniques and behaviors that they have already established. Auditory cueing can be very useful for addressing problems in the categories of knowledge, placement, timing, or musicality. Calling out movements' names at their intended times, advising adjustments in body placement, and clapping along with the steps or singing along with the music to emphasize rhythm or intensity can all be helpful to students "moving in the moment."

For problems with execution, placement, energy, or musicality, offering imagery can be helpful. Kinesthetic, anatomical, visual, and pictorial images can help students determine the correct shape or spatial path of movement, different body parts to engage or release, or feelings to reach for when executing movement.

Finally, videotapes of performance tests are immensely valuable for helping students "see for themselves" specific instances of technical inaccuracy, and for helping teachers suggest corrections.

Identifying Students' Technical and/or Performance Problems

Students learning technique and developing performance sense can benefit immensely from the observations and input of a teacher.

Teachers observe students' execution of movement to analyze their technical correctness, as well as their ability to apply movement principles and work within the rules of the dance form. An overwhelming proportion of teachers' observation time is devoted to looking at technique and its exacting physical rules—the alignment of joints, the correct elevation and placement of the limbs, torso, and head, etc.

Observing and listening simultaneously can allow teachers to gather information about the strength of a student's rhythmic sense and musicality—whether they can match movements with their intended counts and respond to music through movement.

Teachers can look at the movement qualities and energy that students put into movements as a clue to their potential for depth and variety of expression. They can also look for evidence during performance of the synthesis and integration of technical, artistic, and stylistic principles.

Evaluating Students' Solutions to a Given Movement Problem

Problem solving in dance involves the use of movement to accomplish a specific task or communicate a particular intention. Movement problems should be presented at a level appropriate to students' development. They may be as simple as "Find a way to sit on the floor" for inexperienced students, or as complex as "Convey a sense of loss solely through use of the arms" for advanced students. The complexity of other movement problems will be somewhere in between.

The appropriateness of a solution to a movement problem is assessed first on whether it solves the problem, and then on how well it solves it. For example, the teacher could look at how smoothly the sitting motion is achieved, or at how visibly and convincingly the image of loss is conveyed. Teachers can also subjectively assess the creativity with which the student addresses the problem, or the number of different approaches he or she uses to try to find a solution.

Teaching Students Good Time and Resource Management Skills

Resources are scarce in the dance world, and time may be the scarcest resource of all. Long hours in the studio are necessary to develop and maintain technique, as well as learn and rehearse choreography. That time must be balanced with a student's regular schedule, which likely includes school, homework, transportation, extracurricular activities, chores, sleep, and downtime. Often, students can benefit from guidance in how to structure their daily schedules to maximize the use of their time.

Teachers can have students create a breakdown of their daily time usage, as well as daily time requirements and priorities. With this knowledge, students can then create realistic, individualized schedules that will allow them to make the best use of their time each day—and still spend enough time in class and rehearsal.

This scarcity also applies to practice and rehearsal time in the studio. Students may need instruction in how to navigate room schedules and sign-up sheets or online scheduling sites.

Chapter Quiz

Ready to see how well you retained what you just read? Scan the QR code to go directly to the chapter quiz interface for this study guide. If you're using a computer, simply visit the online resources page at **mometrix.com/resources719/aepadance** and click the Chapter Quizzes link.

AEPA Practice Test

Want to take this practice test in an online interactive format?
Check out the online resources page, which includes interactive practice questions and much more: **mometrix.com/resources719/aepadance**

1. The sagittal plane divides the body ______.

a. horizontally
b. diagonally
c. vertically into right and left
d. vertically into front and back

2. In Laban Movement Analysis, the space in which a dancer's body is moving is called the ______.

a. stage
b. ideokinesthetic space
c. kinesphere
d. plane of movement

3. When a *frappé* is performed, the accent is typically on the ______.

a. landing
b. extension of the working leg
c. contraction of the torso
d. turn

4. In Laban's theory of effort (sometimes called movement dynamics), which of the following qualities is not a dimension of effort?

a. Space (direct/indirect)
b. Weight (strong/light)
c. Direction (up/down)
d. Time (sudden/sustained)

Refer to the following for questions 5–6:

Figure 1

5. What is the meter in the waltz depicted in figure 1?

a. 4/3
b. 3/4
c. 6/8
d. Cannot be determined.

6. For which of the following exercises would the music in Figure 1 be most appropriate?

a. Warm-up pliés
b. Fondues at the barre
c. Balancés across the floor
d. Chaînés turns across the floor

7. Which of the following statements correctly describes syncopation?

a. Music with a steady, monotonous beat
b. Music with a 4/4 rhythm
c. Rhythms that deviate from the normal succession of strong and weak beats
d. Rhythms that have a strong Latin influence

8. Which of the following two muscles are used for flexion in dance?

a. Biceps brachii, biceps femoris
b. Biceps brachii, triceps brachii
c. Biceps femoris, adductor magnus
d. Adductor magnus, triceps brachii

Refer to the following for questions 9–10:

Figure 2

1. Begin in fifth position with the right foot in front. 2. Do three *sautés* in fifth position, one *changement*, and then repeat on the left side. 3. Do one *soutenu tournes en dedans* to the right, followed by a single *pirouette en dehors*. Repeat from step one on the opposite side.

9. At what point in a ballet class is the combination described in Figure 2 most likely to be executed?

a. At the *barre*, during warm-up
b. In the center, before warm-up
c. In the center, after warm-up
d. At the end of class, diagonally across the floor

10. If one were to eliminate the jumping elements from the combination described in Figure 2, which steps would be eliminated?

a. The changement only
b. The changement and the sautés
c. The changement, the sautés, and the soutenu tournes en dedans
d. The sautés and the soutenu tournes en dedans

11. The term "*port des bras*" refers to _____.

a. movements of the head
b. movements of the arms
c. movements of the hips
d. movements of the legs

12. Which of the following dance steps is most advanced?

a. *Plié*
b. *Dégagé*
c. *Entrechat*
d. *Tendu*

13. If a ballet step, such as a *grand battement*, is performed *en croix*, this means _____.

a. it is done entirely *en pointe*
b. it is done at an angle to the audience
c. it is done once, then repeated
d. it is performed in all directions

14. It would be most appropriate for a teacher to ask students to perform an exercise incorporating a *grand jeté* at which point in a ballet class?

a. At the barre, immediately following *ronds de jambe*
b. At the barre, immediately following *grand battements*
c. In the center during an adagio exercise
d. At the end of class during an exercise in which the dancers move across the floor

15. A dancer would be likely to use a technique called spotting _____.

a. while executing a pirouette
b. during warm-up *pliés*
c. only while performing on stage
d. while executing a sequence of *grand battements*

16. Which of the following movements can be performed *en dedans*?

a. Pirouette
b. Pas de chat
c. Changement
d. Sauté

17. A dancer is *en pointe* when she is _____.

a. balancing on only one foot
b. balancing on the metatarsal of her foot
c. dancing without the support of the barre
d. balancing on the tip of her toe

18. Which of the following statements is NOT true of modern dance technique?

a. It involves moving off one's center of gravity.
b. It involves contracting the torso.
c. It involves extensive contact with the floor.
d. It has a set of numbered positions for arms and feet.

19. Modern dance rejects all but which of the following tenets of ballet?

a. Legs must always be turned out.
b. Core muscles should always be engaged.
c. Movement quality must always remain light.
d. Arms must almost always remain forward of the torso.

20. Which of the following statements best describes the dance technique introduced by Katherine Dunham?

a. It was purely improvisational and unstructured.
b. It had strong elements of postmodernism.
c. It incorporated elements of African and Caribbean movement.
d. It introduced technology to dance performance.

21. With which of the following styles of modern dance is Isadora Duncan associated?

a. Free dance
b. Modern jazz
c. Ailey jazz
d. Postmodern dance

22. Which of the following steps in tap dance would produce a total of four audible taps?

a. Cramp roll
b. Shuffle
c. Brush
d. Flap

23. Tap dance is known for making heavy use of which of the following types of rhythm?

a. Syncopation
b. Simple meter
c. Polymeter
d. Additive rhythm

24. In jazz dance, bending backward from the knees while maintaining a straight torso is called a ______.

a. hinge
b. contraction
c. isolation
d. back bend

25. Observers would be least likely to see contractions, releases, and isolations in which of the following dance forms?

a. Jazz
b. Modern dance
c. Ballet
d. All of the above

26. The primary purpose of *baile folklórico* is to ______.

a. improve the dancers' physical conditioning
b. display elaborate costumes
c. promote social identity and a sense of community
d. evoke a trance-like state in the dancers

27. Of the following types of social dance listed below, which does not involve partnering?

a. Line dancing
b. Tango
c. Swing dancing
d. Square dancing

28. *Flamenco* dance is ______.

a. a form of dance that originated in Spain and is characterized by audible and often rapid footwork
b. a form of dance that originated in Argentina and that uses music with a 2/4 time signature
c. an ancient, spiritual dance that originated in South India
d. a social dance with Cuban influences that originated in the US and Britain

29. A dance teacher would most likely suggest that a student practice Pilates exercises in order to ______.

a. increase flexibility
b. improve muscle strength
c. improve articulation of the feet
d. improve musicality and spatial awareness

30. Which of the following choices correctly lists the order in which the vertebrae of the spine are arranged, from top to bottom?

a. Cervical, thoracic, lumbar, sacrum, coccyx
b. Coccyx, lumbar, cervical, thoracic, sacrum
c. Lumbar, cervical, thoracic, sacrum, coccyx
d. Cervical, thoracic, sacrum, coccyx, lumbar

31. While executing a *fouetté* turn (*fouetté en tournant*) the dancer's working leg is engaged in ______.

a. flexion and extension
b. elevation and depression
c. plantarflexion and dorsiflexion
d. supination and pronation

32. The hip joint is a ______.

a. saddle joint
b. ball and socket joint
c. hinge joint
d. condyloid joint

33. Which of the following is typically not a goal of ideokinesis?

a. Improving flexibility
b. Improving alignment
c. Achieving relaxation
d. Improving kinesthetic awareness

34. Which of the following statements is not true of proper alignment?

a. It is only necessary in ballet.
b. It builds strength in the core muscles.
c. It improves balance.
d. It prevents injury.

35. If a choreographer requires a ballet dancer to lift another dancer of roughly the same size, how might the dancer who is doing the lifting prepare?

a. No special preparation would be necessary; the upper body strength developed in ballet class would be sufficient.
b. By beginning a weight training program for the upper body.
c. By doing yoga.
d. By doing both Pilates and yoga.

36. In order to relieve muscle tension, a dancer might engage in all but which of the following practices?

a. Pilates
b. Yoga
c. Meditation
d. Ideokinesis

37. Ballet dancers should be encouraged to turn out ______.

a. as far as the ankles will allow
b. as far as the knees will allow
c. as far as the knees will allow and the muscles can support
d. as far as the hips will allow and the muscles can support

38. What is the primary muscle that is stretched by reaching forward from a seated position and bending the upper torso as close to the floor as possible, while the legs are extended to the sides at roughly a 150 degree angle (straddle stretch)?

a. Adductor magnus
b. Biceps femoris
c. Quadriceps
d. Triceps

39. In order to develop a dancer's endurance for a long performance, a teacher would recommend ______.

a. aerobic exercise
b. anaerobic exercise
c. weight training
d. ideokinesis

40. When a dancer suffers a sprain, which of the following would not be an appropriate part of the treatment?

a. Elevating the affected area above the heart.
b. Applying a hot compress such as a heating pad.
c. Compressing the area to reduce swelling.
d. Applying a cold compress such as ice.

41. Tendonitis is typically caused by ______.

a. a fall
b. overstretching a tendon
c. not warming up
d. overuse of a tendon

42. Symptoms of a stress fracture typically include ______.

a. bruising, as well as pain in the affected area, but only at the end of a class
b. tenderness, as well as pain in the affected area that is most intense at the beginning and immediately after a class
c. extreme swelling and pain in the affected area
d. extreme temperature sensitivity in the affected area

43. Dancers' safety is at risk in all but which of the following situations?

a. There are no mirrors in the studio.
b. The studio is excessively cold.
c. The studio is not spacious enough to accommodate the dancers.
d. The floor is not clean and dry.

44. For which of the following types of dance is a shoe with a small, soft heel traditionally worn?

a. Modern
b. Ballet
c. Jazz
d. Lyrical

45. Encouraging dancers to arrive to class on time is most important because ______.

a. it teaches self-discipline
b. it shows respect for the teacher
c. it improves the dancer's focus
d. it ensures that the dancer will participate in the warm-up

46. *Pointe* work ______.

a. can begin at any age, as long as the student has excellent technique
b. should only begin after the bones of the feet are fully formed
c. is traditionally learned by both men and women
d. is only practiced by professional dancers

47. A student who has excessive difficulty balancing, despite following appropriate corrections _____.

a. should not take dance classes
b. may have a vision impairment
c. is definitely distracted by an emotional problem
d. is a danger to other students

48. With regard to nutrition, which of the following is advisable for recreational dance students?

a. Following a restricted-calorie diet
b. Avoiding carbohydrates
c. Consuming approximately the same amount of calories as are burned
d. Consuming more calories than are burned to compensate for those burned while dancing

49. The primary purpose of wearing tight-fitting clothing in dance class is to _____.

a. make dancers self-conscious about their weight
b. make the students' movements more aesthetically pleasing
c. ensure that all dancers are wearing the same "uniform"
d. allow teachers to clearly see the students' alignment and movements

50. A piece of choreography that lacks flow could be improved by the addition of _____.

a. unity
b. transitions
c. adagio
d. variations

51. Phrasing may be determined by all but which of the following?

a. Breath
b. Counts
c. Kinesthetic energy
d. Space

52. Which of the following is an appropriate source for generating choreographic ideas?

a. A bluegrass music composition
b. A play by Shakespeare
c. A dance composition from the post-WWII era
d. All of the above

53. In determining the appropriate type of choreography to present to an audience, the most important information to gather would be _____.

a. the types of dance that the audience members have already been exposed to
b. the age range of the audience members and their previous experiences with theater and dance
c. the style of dance that most audience members prefer
d. the style of music that most audience members prefer

54. In generating new choreography, _____.

a. it is essential to select the music first, and then find movements that fit
b. improvisation can be a useful tool
c. it is important to use only one style or technique
d. the phrasing should always be determined before setting the composition to music

55. Which of the following statements best describes the benefits of live accompaniment for a dance class?

a. Live accompaniment has no benefits; it severely limits the scope of music that can be used in class.
b. Live accompaniment improves dancers' musicality and stage presence.
c. Live accompaniment makes the class go more smoothly because the music can be tailored to the exercises, and teachers can focus on students' performance rather than finding the appropriate music.
d. Live accompaniment improves students' confidence.

56. Nonliteral choreography may have all but which of the following goals?

a. Offering social commentary
b. Telling a traditional story
c. Providing the audience with an aesthetically pleasing experience
d. Evoking emotion in the audience members

57. A choreographer asks four dancers to perform different movements simultaneously. This is called a _____.

a. rondo
b. tableau
c. pantomime
d. ground bass

58. In choreography, the intent of a collage is most likely to _____.

a. produce a sense of comedy or surrealism
b. allow for a set change
c. tell a story
d. showcase both male and female dancers

59. A canon is most likely to be performed _____.

a. by the corps de ballet in Swan Lake
b. during a pas de deux
c. during a jazz or tap solo
d. during a ballet solo

60. In order to remain out of the audience's view until completely entering the stage, a dancer should _____.

a. stay as close as possible to the leg upstage of his or her entrance point
b. stay as close as possible to the leg downstage of his or her entrance point
c. stay away from the lights
d. remain as close to the ground as possible

61. Where is the "apron" of the stage located?

a. At the front, closest to the audience
b. In the orchestra pit
c. "Apron" is another term for "curtain."
d. Between center stage and upstage

62. The inability of dancers to maintain their spacing during a group sequence most likely indicates a lack of ______.

a. musicality
b. kinesthetic awareness
c. flexibility
d. stage presence

63. The most important reason that dancers should rehearse in costume before the performance is that ______.

a. costumes may need to be altered because they do not match the choreographer's intentions
b. the costumes may need to be altered because they do not fit the dancers
c. the costumes may restrict the dancers' movements in ways not anticipated when they were constructed
d. dancers need to determine the appropriate hair and makeup styles to complement the costumes

64. Which of the following statements is not true of the role of facial expression in dance?

a. It is sometimes dictated by choreography.
b. It should be minimized so as not to distract from the choreography.
c. It enhances the audience's enjoyment of the choreography.
d. It needs to be practiced along with the choreography.

65. Which of the following tasks is the duty of a stage manager?

a. Selling and collecting tickets
b. Painting the sets
c. Coordinating lighting and sound cues
d. Rehearsing the dancers

66. Which of the following do Bharatanatyam and liturgical dance have in common?

a. They both originated in India.
b. They are both forms of sacred dance.
c. They both involve rapid spinning to evoke a state of trance.
d. They are both national dances.

67. Which of the following statements correctly describes a commonality between traditional European folk dance and hip-hop dance in the United States?

a. Both originated in the upper socioeconomic class and were later adopted by the socioeconomically disadvantaged.
b. Both were developed exclusively by racial minorities.
c. Both originated as forms of social dance.
d. Both are traditionally performed in lines.

68. The accomplishments of dancers/choreographers like William Henry "Master Juba" Lane, Savion Glover, Katherine Dunham, and Alvin Ailey exemplify _____.

a. the contribution of African-Americans to dance
b. musical theater's influence on jazz and modern dance
c. the importance of learning ballet along with jazz or modern
d. the value of drawing choreographic inspiration from poetry

69. Which of the following is an example of dance challenging traditional gender roles in society?

a. A man leading a woman in the tango.
b. A male dancer partnering a female dancer in a pas des deux.
c. A female dancer lifting a male dancer in a modern piece.
d. A woman performing belly dancing in the Middle East.

70. Which of the following societal changes has probably had the least impact on the variety of dance styles that are performed in the United States today?

a. Globalization
b. Economic development
c. The Civil Rights and women's rights movements
d. Immigration

71. Which of the following ballets used music not composed by Tchaikovsky?

a. Giselle
b. Swan Lake
c. The Nutcracker
d. The Sleeping Beauty

72. Which of the following is not true of Romantic ballets?

a. They are characterized by an emphasis on the appearance of defying gravity.
b. They contain heavy use of pantomiming.
c. They reached their peak popularity in the 19th century.
d. They introduced the ballerina, as opposed to the male dancer, as a central part of the performance.

73. Early modern dance composition, such as that of Martha Graham, was characterized by which of the following forms?

a. Romantic
b. Narrative
c. Nonliteral
d. Geometric

74. A repertoire is _____.

a. the complete list of dance compositions that a group or company is prepared to perform
b. the list of major influences on a particular choreographer's work
c. all of the pieces composed by a particular choreographer or composer
d. all of the steps that a dancer is capable of performing

75. Which of the following men is known for pioneering tap dance as a young man living in the Five Points neighborhood of New York City?

a. William Henry "Master Juba" Lane
b. Merce Cunningham
c. Fred Astaire
d. Howard "Sandman" Simms

76. Ballet uses the French language because ______.

a. although Russians invented ballet, they deeply admired French culture and adopted its language
b. up until the beginning of the 20th century, only the French performed ballet
c. early ballet performers believed that only the French language could accurately express the grace of this dance form
d. many ballet steps were introduced and named in the French court of Louis the XIV

77. The jazz dance choreography in the musical theater classics *Chicago* and *Cabaret* is the work of ______.

a. Bob Fosse
b. Alvin Ailey
c. Katherine Dunham
d. Jerome Robbins

78. In evaluating the choreography in a performance, which of the following types of information would be most useful?

a. Knowing how long the dancers have been rehearsing
b. Understanding the expectations of the audience
c. Knowing how large the budget for the performance was
d. Knowing the intent of the choreographer

79. When evaluating dance performances, it is important to understand the historical context because ______.

a. the cultural or social significance of the composition may not be clear to those unfamiliar with the historical context
b. knowing the historical context should improve the aesthetic quality of the performance
c. it suggests how old the dancers would be if they were alive today
d. it explains how the particular dance technique in question emerged

80. As opposed to a dance critic, an audience member is ______.

a. more likely to evaluate a performance based on its technical merits
b. less likely to criticize a dance performance for being derivative
c. more likely to appreciate references to dance history
d. more likely to appreciate original choreography

81. Why would original choreography be more important in a contemporary dance concert than in a performance of *The Nutcracker*?

a. This fits with audience members' expectations.
b. The costumes and sets for contemporary dance concerts are less elaborate, so original choreography is necessary to add interest.
c. Performers in The Nutcracker are usually more technically proficient.
d. Contemporary dance concerts have a greater range of choreographic options.

82. Asking students to research a non-Western culture and perform a dance from that culture is an example of an _________ approach to learning.

a. interdisciplinary
b. atypical
c. interrelated
d. isolated

83. Which of the following describes a way in which language arts could be integrated into a dance class?

a. Asking students to count the beats aloud
b. Explaining to students how the hip joint works
c. Reading a poem and asking students to improvise a short dance inspired by it
d. All of the above

84. Which of the following examples highlights a way in which music and dance composition are similar?

a. Both can only be done by professionals.
b. Each must be done with the other in mind.
c. Both may rely on improvisation.
d. Neither can be done during a performance.

85. A dance teacher gives each student two minutes to individually compose and perform a combination of steps in front of the dance class. Which of the following skills is this exercise most directly designed to teach?

a. Identifying relationships between dance and other fine art subjects
b. Developing sensitivity toward others when working in groups
c. Performing memorized movement sequences with rhythmical accuracy
d. Improvising and demonstrating original movement

86. The best way for a teacher to teach a new sequence of steps to a class composed of visual and kinesthetic learners would be to ______.

a. demonstrate the exercise
b. demonstrate the exercise while describing it aloud
c. describe the exercise aloud and ask students to do the steps as the teacher says them
d. demonstrate the exercise and allow students to practice it along with the teacher

87. Videotaping a class and then asking the students to watch their performance ______.

a. is a bad idea because students may feel uncomfortable watching themselves
b. may help students identify new areas to improve, or to understand the teacher's corrections better
c. is a dangerous distraction
d. would be especially useful for very young children

88. Which of the following activities would be least likely to improve metacognitive skills?

a. Giving an oral presentation about dance history
b. Solving a choreographic problem while verbalizing one's thought process
c. Explaining the solution to a choreographic problem to another student
d. Explaining the solution to a choreographic problem in writing

89. Dance teachers need both pedagogical and content knowledge in order to succeed. Which of the following is an example of pedagogical knowledge?

a. Understanding how to plan and execute a stage production
b. Knowing how to properly assess students' progress
c. Being familiar with the social and cultural history of dance
d. Knowing how to correctly execute movement sequences

90. A research and writing assignment would be most appropriate for assessing which of the following skills?

a. Demonstrating basic kinesthetic and spatial awareness of others
b. Demonstrating basic principles of proper skeletal alignment
c. Comparing and contrasting the use of form and expression in dance with their use in art, music, theater, and other subject areas
d. Incorporating injury prevention procedures when exercising, practicing, and performing

91. For a ballet class that lasts 90 minutes, which of the following choices represents the best way to structure the class?

a. 5 minutes at the barre, 80 minutes in the center, and 5 minutes across the floor
b. 15 minutes at the center, 15 minutes at the barre, and one hour across the floor
c. 30 minutes at the barre, 40 minutes in the center, and 20 minutes across the floor
d. 80 minutes at the barre, 5 minutes in the center, and 5 minutes across the floor

92. The best way for a teacher to handle a class with beginning, intermediate, and advanced students would be to ______.

a. focus only on the beginning students and let the advanced students take care of themselves
b. focus only on the advanced students since they have the most potential
c. target all exercises to the intermediate level
d. demonstrate versions of each exercise that are appropriate for the various levels

93. While a class is performing an exercise, the teacher notices that several students are having a similar problem with technique. The best way to address this problem would be to _____.

a. use imagery to explain the difference between the proper and improper technique
b. ask a student who is performing the movement correctly to demonstrate it
c. correct the students who are performing the movement incorrectly by physically manipulating their bodies into the correct position, as long as this would be safe
d. use all of the above methods, or as many as possible

94. How can the Body Mass Index (BMI) measure help a teacher determine whether a student is overweight or underweight?

a. BMI is not useful because it only considers a person's weight.
b. It is helpful because it can convert measurements in kilograms into measurements in pounds.
c. It is helpful because it indicates whether a student's weight is proportional to his or her height.
d. It is helpful because it indicates a person's ratio of fat to muscle.

95. To make the combination described in Figure 3 more appropriate for technically advanced dancers, a teacher might _____.

Figure 3

1. Begin in fifth position with the right foot in front.
2. Do two *assemblés en dedans*, followed by four *changements*.
3. Do two *glissades changé* to the right, followed by a *pirouette en dehors*.

Repeat from step one on the opposite side.

a. eliminate the changements
b. change the changements to entrechats
c. ask dancers to execute the jumps in third position instead of fifth position
d. ask the dancers to do the combination twice

96. In order to improve students' kinesthetic awareness and originality, a teacher might assign _____.

a. a contact improvisation exercise
b. a barre exercise
c. a weight training regimen
d. ideokinesis exercises

97. A written test would be an ideal assessment tool for which of the following skills?

a. Developing sensitivity toward others when working in groups
b. Identifying historical figures and their significance in dance history
c. Performing basic compositional forms using fundamental choreographic processes
d. Expressing ideas and emotions through movement

98. For the following skill, what would be the best assessment method? "The student is expected to perform dance phrases or dances from several time periods with an understanding of historical and social contexts."

a. Written test supplemented by a performance-based assessment
b. Group-based performance assessment
c. Research project
d. Performance-based assessment only

99. Rubrics are most effective for ______.

a. improving metacognitive skills
b. helping students to formulate long-term goals
c. assessing complex assignments
d. teaching critical thinking

100. In order to evaluate students' ability to "demonstrate appropriate audience behavior and etiquette in the classroom and at performances," the most effective assessment method would be to ______.

a. ask students to choreograph and present a performance to friends and family
b. discuss appropriate audience behavior during class
c. give students a test with questions about appropriate audience behavior
d. explain appropriate audience behavior, and then take students to a performance and evaluate their behavior there

Answer Key and Explanations

1. C: In anatomy, the body is divided by three planes, including the sagittal plane that divides it vertically into a right and left side. Choice A refers to the transverse (horizontal) plane, D refers to the frontal plane, and the diagonal plane mentioned in B does not exist in anatomy.

2. C: In Laban Movement Analysis, the immediate space in which a dancer's body is moving is called the kinesphere, or reach space.

3. B: When a *frappé* is performed, the accent is typically on the extension of the working leg. A *frappé* involves a strong, quick (accented) extension of the leg from a *sur le coup de pied* position. This step does not involve jumping and landing (A), turning (D), or contracting the torso (C).

4. C: Direction is not a dimension of effort in movement dynamics. According to Laban, the four dimensions of effort are space, weight, time, and flow.

5. B: The meter, or time signature, is always shown at the beginning of the musical score, usually following the key signature or the clef. It describes the number of beats per measure, and it is read from top to bottom, which means that choice A is incorrect because the numbers are reversed. If C were correct, the meter would show a six at the top and an eight at the bottom.

6. C: The music in Figure A, a waltz, would be most appropriate for *balancés* across the floor. Unlike the other choices, *balancés* are a movement in three beats, making the time signature of a waltz particularly appropriate for this exercise.

7. C: Syncopation is best described as any rhythm that deviates from the normal succession of strong and weak beats. Music with a steady, monotonous beat (A) would lack the deviations that characterize syncopation, and B (music with a 4/4 rhythm) and D (rhythms that have a strong Latin influence) describe types of music that may or may not be syncopated.

8. A: Both the biceps brachii (located above the front of the elbow) and biceps femoris (hamstrings) engage in flexion (decreasing the angle between two bones). In other words, the biceps brachii bends the arm, and the biceps femoris helps to bend the leg. The adductor magnus brings the legs together and also helps to extend the leg. The triceps brachii is used to extend the arm.

9. C: The combination described in Figure 2 would usually be executed in the center, after warm-up. Because it contains jumps and turns, it should not be attempted during or before warm-up (A and B), and it would not be done diagonally across the floor, because it moves right to left, rather than in a straight line.

10. B: If one were to eliminate the jumping elements from the combination described in Figure 2, the *changement* and the *sautés* would be removed. The *soutenu tournes en dedans* and the *pirouette* would remain, as these are both turns.

11. B: The term "*port des bras*" refers to movements of the arms, and also to a movement that involves bending the torso in any direction.

12. C: An *entrechat* is the most advanced step listed here. *Pliés*, *tendus*, and *dégagés* are all beginner level steps in ballet, while an *entrechat* is a more advanced jump.

13. D: If a ballet step is performed *en croix*, this means it is performed in all directions (*devant, a la seconde, derrière*, and *a la seconde* again). This is often the case for *tendus, dégagés*, and *grand battements*.

14. D: It would be most appropriate for a teacher to ask students to perform an exercise incorporating a *grand jeté* at the end of class during an exercise in which the dancers move across the floor. *Grand jeté* is a leap that involves taking off from one foot, attaining a split midair, and landing on the alternate foot. Because of the horizontal and vertical distance traveled during this movement, choices A and B are both incorrect; it would be impractical to execute a *grand jeté* at the barre. It would also be unsafe to attempt such a movement before completing the warm-up at the barre. Choice C is incorrect because adagio exercises involve slow, sustained movements, and the *grand jeté* clearly does not fit into this category.

15. A: A dancer would be likely to use a technique called spotting while executing a pirouette. Spotting involves looking at a single spot for as long as possible while the body turns and then snapping the head around to find that same spot again as the body returns to its starting place. It is used to maintain focus and to alleviate dizziness while turning. Spotting is used any time a turn is executed, not just on stage (C), and it is not necessary during *pliés* or *grand battements* (B and D) because these steps do not involve turning.

16. A: A *pirouette* is the only step of the four listed that can be performed *en dedans*. This term describes motions in which the leg moves from the rear of the body to the front of the body in a roundabout motion, and can be used to describe *ronds de jambe* as well as *pirouettes*. The *pas de chat* cannot be performed *en dedans* because the feet remain beneath the body's center of gravity during this step, and it does not necessarily entail moving the back foot to the forward position. While the *changement* does require the back foot to move to the forward position, this change is executed with the feet in fifth or third position, always directly below the center of gravity. *Sautés* do not involve moving the back foot forward at all.

17. D: A dancer is *en pointe* when she is balancing on the tip of her toe, using special *pointe* shoes. When a dancer balances on the metatarsal of her foot (B), this is called *demi-pointe*, and choices A (balancing on only one foot) and C (dancing without the support of the *barre*) can be done *en pointe* or *demi-pointe*.

18. D: All of these statements are true of modern dance technique except that it does not have a set of numbered positions for arms and feet like ballet does.

19. B: Modern dance technique does not require that legs always be turned out (A), that movement quality always remain light (C), or that arms always remain forward of the torso (D). However, proper execution does require that core muscles always be engaged.

20. C: Katherine Dunham's style incorporated elements of African and Caribbean movement into modern dance. While her movement style is certainly less structured than ballet, it is typically choreographed ahead of time and not improvised during the performance like free dance, so choice A is incorrect. Dunham's technique pre-dated postmodernism and the dance technology movement (B and D).

21. A: Isadora Duncan is associated with free dance, which was the earliest manifestation of modern dance. Free dance rejected the rigidity of classical ballet, and served as a precursor to the other types of modern dance listed here.

22. A: A cramp roll involves stepping first onto one metatarsal, then onto the other (two taps), and then dropping the first and then the second heel to the floor. The other steps in choices B, C, and D all involve only one or two audible sounds.

23. A: Tap dance is known for making heavy use of syncopation, or a rhythmic style that deviates from the expected pattern of strong and weak beats. One of the expected patterns is simple meter (B). Polymeter (C) is incorrect because it is characterized by two unrelated rhythms playing simultaneously. Additive rhythm (D) is incorrect because it refers to a longer meter that is used in many non-Western styles of music.

24. A: In jazz dance, bending backward from the knees while maintaining a straight torso is called a hinge. A contraction (B) involves a strong forward curvature of the torso and hips, an isolation (C) involves moving only one body part at a time, and a back bend (D) involves arching the back, as opposed to keeping it straight.

25. C: Observers would be least likely to see contractions, releases, and isolations in ballet. Isolations involve moving just one part of the body at a time and are a staple of jazz dance. Contractions and releases are common in modern dance, but they are rare in ballet because it almost inevitably requires an upright posture that simulates lightness. Contractions involve curving the upper body, and releases often involve a sudden relaxation of certain muscles, which gives the movement a "heavy" quality.

26. C: The primary purpose of *baile folklórico* is to promote social identity and a sense of community. While it may also improve the dancers' physical conditioning (A) or involve costumes (B), *baile folklórico* is primarily a social dance that is done for pleasure and as a way of experiencing and sharing culture. It is not intended to evoke a trance-like state in the dancers (D).

27. A: Line dancing does not involve partnering. Instead of being performed by couples, line dancing is performed in one or several lines. This is similar to the way that traditional folk dances are performed, except that line dancing is more individualized and usually does not involve contact between adjoining dancers. The other three types of social dance listed here, including tango, swing dance, and square dance, are all performed by couples.

28. A: *Flamenco* is a form of dance that originated in Spain and is characterized by audible and often rapid footwork. Choice B refers to the tango, C refers to Bharatanatyam, and D refers to the rhumba, a type of ballroom dance.

29. B: Pilates is most often assigned to improve a dancer's muscle strength, particularly core muscle strength. Although there is some evidence that Pilates may improve flexibility (A), this is not the main purpose of these exercises. Similarly, Pilates exercises do not directly target the feet (C), and are not usually performed to music (D).

30. A: The term for the seven vertebrae at the top of the spine is "cervical." These cervical vertebrae are located just above twelve thoracic vertebrae, five lumbar vertebrae, five bones in the sacrum, and three to five bones in the coccyx.

31. A: The working leg (the leg that is not supporting the body's weight) is engaged in flexion and extension during a *fouetté*. Flexion and extension involves increasing or decreasing the angle between two bones, in this case the upper and lower bones of the leg. Elevation and depression (B) involve raising and lowering the scapula (shoulder blade), plantarflexion and dorsiflexion (C) involve extending and flexing the ankle, and supination and pronation (D) involve rotating the palm upward or downward. During a *fouetté*, the ankle of the standing (not working) leg engages in plantarflexion and dorsiflexion.

32. B: The hip joint is a ball and socket joint. A saddle joint (A), like the thumb, is opposable, meaning it moves in two planes. Hinge joints (C), like the elbow or knee, move along only one plane. Condyloid joints (D) move along two planes like saddle joints, but they are shaped differently. The wrist is an example of a condyloid joint.

33. A: Improving flexibility is typically not a goal of ideokinesis. Ideokinesis involves imagining muscle movement, and has been shown to activate muscles even when the movement being imagined is not actually being executed. Ideokinesis is good for improving alignment (B) and kinesthetic awareness (D) because it allows dancers to mentally "practice"; it has also been shown to facilitate muscle relaxation (C).

34. A: Proper alignment is necessary in all types of dance, not just ballet. It builds strength in the core muscles (B), improves balance (C), and prevents injuries that arise from improper alignment (D).

35. B: If a choreographer requires a ballet dancer to lift another dancer of roughly the same size, beginning a weight training program for the upper body would be appropriate. While yoga and Pilates do help develop strength, they consist only of weight-bearing exercise; the dancer must train to bear nearly as much or more than his or her own weight.

36. A: Pilates, unlike yoga, meditation, and ideokinesis, is not intended to relieve tension. Its primary goal is to build strength and improve kinesthetic awareness.

37. D: Ballet dancers should be encouraged to turn out only as far as the hips will allow and the muscles can support. Turning out from the knees or ankles distorts technique and can cause injury. Turnout should always be initiated from the muscles in the hips and thighs, and the lower leg should never be forced to turn out more than the upper leg.

38. A: This exercise primarily stretches the adductor magnus, the muscle that runs along the inside of the leg from the knee to the groin area.

39. A: To develop a dancer's endurance for a long performance, a teacher would recommend aerobic exercise. Unlike anaerobic exercise, which increases one's ability to deliver strength and power in short bursts, aerobic exercise improves the body's ability to deliver oxygen to muscles during long periods of sustained activity. Although most dance classes involve a combination of aerobic and anaerobic exercise (a *barre* warm-up with few breaks would be aerobic, but a one-minute jumping combination followed by a break would be anaerobic), the best way to improve lung capacity and endurance for long performances is aerobic exercise. While weight training and ideokinesis are excellent ways to develop other skills, they are not sufficient to increase endurance.

40. B: A confirmed sprain should be treated with rest, ice (D), compression (C), and elevation (A), but heat (B) is not an advisable treatment for a sprain.

41. D: Tendonitis is typically caused by over-using a particular muscle and the associated tendon. Falling (A) may cause other injuries such as sprains or fractures, but not tendonitis. Overstretching a muscle may damage the muscle, but tendons themselves are very difficult to stretch (B); if they do become stretched, this increases the risk of sprains, but not tendonitis. Not warming up (C) properly can also lead to muscle damage, but this is not a direct cause of tendonitis.

42. B: Symptoms of a stress fracture typically include tenderness, as well as pain in the affected area that is most intense at the beginning and immediately after a class. Bruising and swelling usually do not occur, nor does temperature sensitivity.

43. A: Mirrors are a pedagogical tool and are not central to dancers' safety. However, dancers' safety is at risk if the studio is too cold because this can cause muscle injuries. Studios that are too small can be dangerous because dancers may inadvertently collide, causing serious injury. Dirty, slippery, or wet floors can cause dangerous falls as well.

44. C: Modern dance is usually done barefoot, ballet slippers do not have heels, and jazz sandals are usually worn for lyrical dance.

45. D: Encouraging dancers to arrive to class on time is most important because it ensures that the dancer will participate in the warm-up. While arriving to class on time also teaches self-discipline (A), shows respect for the teacher (B), and improves the dancer's focus (C), arriving on time is most important because missing even part of the warm-up can cause injury.

46. B: *Pointe* work should only begin after the bones of the feet are fully formed. Choice A is incorrect because even for young dancers with excellent technique, serious bone deformities can result from starting *pointe* too early. C is incorrect because traditionally only women perform *en pointe*, and D is incorrect because amateur dancers may also learn to perform *pointe* work, as long as they are old enough and have learned appropriate ballet technique.

47. B: A student who has excessive difficulty balancing, despite following appropriate corrections, may have vision impairment. Students who appear to be using proper technique, but still have trouble balancing and turning, may be suffering from a vision problem that, if corrected, could improve their performance in class.

48. C: It is advisable for recreational dance students to consume approximately the same amount of calories as are burned. Following a restricted-calorie diet (A) can lead to health problems, as can avoiding any major food group like carbohydrates (B). Dancers only need to consume the same number of calories as they burn, including those burned while dancing (D). Eating more calories than are burned can cause weight gain, even among those who participate in physical activity like dance classes, and this can put students at risk for obesity.

49. D: The primary purpose of wearing tight-fitting clothing in dance class is to allow teachers to clearly see the students' alignment and movements. If clothing is baggy, teachers may have difficulty seeing and correcting problems. While some teachers think that it is important for all students to wear the same "uniform" to class, requiring tight-fitting clothing alone does not achieve this end. While A and B may result from requiring fitted attire in class, they are either unwanted side effects of this practice in the case of A, or in the case of B, a secondary benefit.

50. B: A piece of choreography that lacks flow could be improved by the addition of transitions. Flow involves the existence of logical connections between steps, and transitions are the connective tissue that leads a dancer from one step to another without having each step appear isolated. Unity (A) refers to the thematic coherence of a piece of choreography, and the term "variation" (D) usually refers to specific pieces of choreography within a larger work. *Adagio* (C) refers to slow, sustained movement or music.

51. D: Phrases, the smaller subunits that make up a dance, can be marked by the length of time it takes a dancer to inhale or exhale (A). They can also be marked by a count system (i.e., eight counts equals one phrase) (B), or by the time it takes for an initial burst of kinesthetic energy to expire (C). Space would not be an effective way to mark temporal sections of a dance.

52. D: All of the sources described here, including music, plays, and pre-existing dance compositions, are excellent sources of ideas for generating new choreography.

53. B: In determining the appropriate type of choreography to present to an audience, the most important information to gather would be the age range of the audience members and their previous experiences with theater and dance. While it may be useful to know the styles of dance (C) and music (D) that most audience members prefer, this knowledge should not restrict the choreographer to choosing that particular type of dance or music since expanding the horizons of the audience is an important role of the choreographer. Additionally, it may be useful to know what types of dance the audience has already been exposed to (A), but the best answer is (B) because this choice also takes into account the age range of the audience. Certain themes may be inappropriate for children or families, for example, and choreographers may want to introduce more complex and challenging choreography to audiences that have a more sophisticated understanding of dance.

54. B: In generating new choreography, improvisation can be a useful tool. Neither choice A nor D is correct because there is no set rule regarding the order in which the music and movement should be chosen. C is incorrect because, while it may be helpful to have a single style or technique in mind, the infusion of elements from various styles can enrich and add interest to a composition.

55. C: Live accompaniment makes the class go more smoothly because the music can be tailored to the exercises, and teachers can focus on students' performance rather than finding the appropriate music. There is no particular reason to think that live accompaniment has any advantage over recorded music where students' confidence (D) or musicality (B) is concerned, and it is untrue that live accompaniment has no benefits whatsoever (A).

56. B: Unlike literal choreography, which tells a story, nonliteral choreography is intended to communicate directly to the audience through movement.

57. B: When dancers perform different movements simultaneously, this is called a tableau. Ground bass (D) involves repetition of one movement theme as other contrasting themes are brought forward. A rondo (A) is a choreographic form in which, much like verse and chorus, a repeated theme is alternated with varying themes in between. Pantomime (C) involves gesturing to express a specific verbal concept.

58. A: In choreography, the intent of a collage is most likely to produce a sense of irony or surrealism. A collage involves the juxtaposition of incongruous elements, sometimes to create a dreamlike effect.

59. A: A canon involves a group of dancers performing the same movement one after the other, and thus would most likely be performed by the *corps de ballet* in *Swan Lake*. The other options all refer to types of choreography that only include one or two dancers, and it would not be practical to choreograph a canon without multiple dancers.

60. B: In order to remain out of the audience's view until completely entering the stage, a dancer should stay as close as possible to the leg downstage of his or her entrance point. Legs, the large sheets of fabric that are hung alongside the stage in order to allow the dancers to wait for their cue without being seen by the audience, only provide partial coverage. Dancers must stay as close as possible to the wing downstage of their entrance point because staying as far upstage as possible (A) would allow them to be seen marginally sooner.

61. A: The "apron" is located at the front of the stage. When dancers enter this area, they become very difficult to see, especially for audience members in the front. The area is usually marked by different flooring or tape.

62. B: The inability of dancers to maintain their spacing in a group sequence most likely indicates a lack of kinesthetic awareness. Kinesthetic awareness refers to an individual's sense and understanding of the location of his or her body relative to other bodies and objects in space and of how his or her muscles are moving. Musicality (A), flexibility (C), and stage presence (D) may be important to the successful execution of group choreography, but they do not directly affect the dancers' awareness of their spacing (positioning relative to one another). Spacing can be maintained even when dancers are not precisely on the music.

63. C: While each of these four answers may be correct, the most important reason that dancers should rehearse in costume before the performance is that the costumes may restrict the dancers' movements in ways not anticipated when they were constructed (C). Dancers must rehearse in the costumes to identify and address any movement restrictions or other problems that seem likely to cause injury or to prevent the choreography from being executed as planned.

64. B: Of the three statements above, "facial expression should be minimized so as not to distract from the choreography," is the only false one. Choreographers typically select specific facial expressions for dancers to complement their choreography (A), and coach dancers on this during rehearsals (D). Facial expressions, like the choreography itself, are selected to enhance the audience's enjoyment (C).

65. C: Stage managers are responsible for coordinating non-dance aspects of a performance, such as lighting, sound, sets, and props. The house manager is responsible for selling and collecting tickets (A), and although the stage manager might coordinate the construction, placement, and changing of sets, a stagehand would typically be responsible for painting them (B). Directors are usually in charge of rehearsing the dancers (D), as a stage manager's expertise is in the technical aspects of stagecraft, rather than dance itself.

66. B: Bharatanatyam and liturgical dance are both forms of sacred dance. Choice A is incorrect because although Bharatanatyam originated in India, liturgical dance is a Western Christian tradition. Neither type of dance involves rapid spinning to evoke a state of trance (C); this is a reference to the dervishes of the Middle East. Last, while Bharatanatyam is considered by some to be a national dance of India, liturgical dance is not typically considered an expression of national identity in any Western nation (D).

67. C: Both emerged as forms of social dance. Choice A is incorrect because the reverse is true; both European folk dance and hip-hop were pioneered by individuals who were socioeconomically disadvantaged, and B is incorrect because, although hip-hip was developed by racial minorities in the US, this was not the case for most European folk dances. D is incorrect because, although many European folk dances are performed in lines, this is not the norm for hip-hop.

68. A: The accomplishments of dancers/choreographers like William Henry "Master Juba" Lane, Savion Glover, Katherine Dunham, and Alvin Ailey exemplify the contribution of African-Americans to dance. Lane and Glover have been pioneers in tap dance, and Dunham and Ailey introduced African and Caribbean influences to modern dance and jazz.

69. C: A female dancer lifting a male dancer in a modern piece is an example of dance challenging traditional gender roles in society because it contradicts both the classical ballet tradition of men lifting women and also symbolically rejects the societal tradition of viewing women as dependent upon and subservient to men. The examples in choices A and B, a man leading a woman in the tango and a male dancer partnering a female dancer in a *pas des deux*, both reinforce traditional gender roles. Although belly dancing is viewed by some women in the West as a liberating, empowering experience, belly dancing in the Middle East is a practice representative of traditional gender roles.

70. B: Economic development has probably had the least impact on the variety of dance styles that are performed in the United States today. Globalization (A) and immigration (D) have popularized many dance styles from around the world (for example, Irish dancing and belly dancing), and the Civil Rights and women's rights movements allowed previously marginalized individuals like Isadora Duncan, Martha Graham, Katherine Dunham, Alvin Ailey, and William Henry "Master Juba" Lane to pioneer new styles of dance like modern dance, tap dance, and African-Caribbean dance.

71. A: The music for *Giselle* was composed by Adolphe Adam. All others were composed by Russian composer Peter Illych Tchaikovsky.

72. B: Romantic ballets do not contain heavy use of pantomiming, which refers to the use of gestures to express concepts. Romantic ballets like *La Sylphide* and *Giselle* were characterized by an emphasis on the appearance of defying gravity (A), reached their peak popularity in the 19th century (C), and introduced the ballerina as a central part of the performance (D).

73. B: These early works typically told a story using literal, rather than nonliteral choreography (C). They were not Romantic (A), as this term is typically associated with a specific era in ballet that used very different costuming and movement styles from that adopted by early modern dancers. Geometric (D) styles involve forming intentionally geometric patterns with the dancers' bodies, and this was not a theme in early modern dance.

74. A: A repertoire is the complete list of dance compositions that a group or company is prepared to perform. For example, *The Nutcracker* is a part of almost every ballet company's repertoire.

75. A: William Henry "Master Juba" Lane is known as the originator of tap dance. Fred Astaire (C) and Howard "Sandman" Simms (D) were famous tap dancers from a later era, and Merce Cunningham (B) is a well-known modern dancer and choreographer who worked with Martha Graham.

76. D: Ballet uses the French language because many ballet steps were introduced and named in the French court of Louis the XIV. While Russian ballet dancers did use French ballet vocabulary (A), they did not invent the art form, but rather imported it from France along with the vocabulary. Choice B is incorrect because ballet was already practiced across the Western world by the beginning of the 20th century, and C is incorrect because French was chosen for its utility (i.e., it was the language of the practitioners), not necessarily its beauty.

77. A: Alvin Ailey and Katherine Dunham are both celebrated modern dancers and choreographers whose work incorporates strong African and Caribbean elements, and Jerome Robbins is a jazz choreographer best known for *West Side Story* and *Fiddler on the Roof.*

78. D: Knowing the intent of the choreographer would be the most useful type of information for someone attempting to evaluate the choreography in a performance. Choreography is most effectively evaluated on its own terms (i.e., by comparing the intended effect to the actual effect that was produced). The other options might be important contextual factors for evaluating the quality of the dancers' performance, the audience's reaction, or technical aspects of the performance.

79. A: When evaluating historical dance performances, it is important to understand the historical context because the cultural or social significance of the composition may not be clear to those not familiar with the context. Aesthetic enjoyment is largely personal and emotional, so it would not be enhanced by factual knowledge about the historical context, and this knowledge may or may not explain how the particular dance technique in question emerged.

80. B: Compared to a dance critic, an audience member is less likely to criticize a dance performance for being derivative. Based on the typical assumption that an audience member has less experience and training in dance, an audience member is less likely to notice and appreciate references to dance history (C) or original choreography (D). While audience members are more likely to focus excessively on the technical aspects of a performance (A), they are less likely to notice that particular elements of a performance are derivative (unoriginal).

81. A: Original choreography would be more important in a contemporary dance concert than in a performance of *The Nutcracker* because audience members attend these two types of performances with fundamentally different expectations. *The Nutcracker* is a traditional ballet that is usually targeted at families and individuals who do not necessarily spend a lot of time watching or learning about dance. In contrast to *The Nutcracker*, a ballet in which the audience is expecting pure entertainment, audience members who attend a contemporary dance concert expect to see new and original work.

82. A: Asking students to research a non-Western culture and perform a dance from that culture is an example of an interdisciplinary approach to learning because it combines dance education with another subject, social studies. Interrelated approaches (C) to learning emphasize commonalities between art forms.

83. C: Reading a poem and asking students to improvise a short dance inspired by it is a way that language arts could be integrated into a dance class. Asking students to count the beats aloud (A) would integrate math into the class, and explaining how the hip joint works (B) is an example of integrating science or health into the class.

84. C: Music and dance composition are similar in that both processes may rely on improvisation. Both can be done by amateurs or professionals (A), and both dance and music can be composed without reference to the other. Last, improvisation of music composition and dance choreography can both occur during performances. In music, this is especially common in jazz performances, and it is also common in tap dance and modern dance performances.

85. D: This exercise is designed to help students develop the skill of improvising and demonstrating original movement. Since the students are working alone, rather than in groups, choice B is incorrect, as is A, since students are not assigned to integrate their performance with music or any other aspect of the fine arts. Last, since the students are not using music or memorizing a sequence beforehand, C is incorrect.

86. D: In order to teach a new sequence of steps to a class composed of both visual and kinesthetic learners, the teacher would need to demonstrate the exercise for the visual learners (those who learn by watching) and allow kinesthetic learners (those who learn by doing) to practice the exercise themselves. Just demonstrating the exercise (A) would only appeal to the visual learners, and demonstrating the exercise while describing it aloud (B) would only appeal to visual and auditory learners (those who learn by listening). The method described in choice C would appeal to auditory and kinesthetic learners, but not visual learners.

While learning styles do vary some from person to person, all people do need learn from visual information, auditory information, and by hands-on learning. Different materials lend themselves to a different format, but where possible, the best practice when presenting information to others is to use a mixture of formats, including hands-on materials, visual, and auditory information to keep the materials engaging to all learners.

87. B: Videotaping a class and then asking the students to watch their performance may help students identify new areas to improve, or to understand the teacher's corrections better. Since the teacher can only focus on a certain number of students and make a certain number of corrections during the exercise, occasionally videotaping a class can help students and teachers identify and address problem areas. Choice C is incorrect because the video camera would be unobtrusive, and A is incorrect because dance students need to become accustomed to being observed while they dance. D is also incorrect, since young children would lack the attention span and sophistication for this exercise.

88. A: Giving an oral presentation would be least likely to improve metacognitive skills. Metacognitive skills involve one's ability to "think about thinking," and the other three choices, solving a problem while verbalizing one's thought process (B), explaining the solution to a problem to another student (C), and explaining the solution to a problem in writing (D), all require the student to make the thought process explicit. An oral presentation would not fall into this category because it involves presenting a finished intellectual product, rather than observing and/or analyzing its development.

89. B: Knowing how to properly assess students' progress is an example of pedagogical knowledge. Content knowledge is kinesthetic and/or factual knowledge of the subject being taught—for example, knowing how to plan and execute a stage production (A), being familiar with the social and cultural history of dance (C), and knowing how to correctly execute movement sequences (D). Pedagogical knowledge refers to an understanding of the most effective processes and methods of imparting one's content knowledge to others.

90. C: A research and writing assignment would be most appropriate for assessing a dance student's ability to compare and contrast the use of form and expression in dance with their use in art, music, theater, and other subject areas. Since the other choices all involve practical actions and behaviors, they cannot be properly assessed using a research paper.

91. C: 30 minutes at the *barre*, 40 minutes in the center, and 20 minutes across the floor. Although this structure does not have to be followed exactly, and slightly more or less time may be spent on any given part of the class, choice C represents the most appropriate use of time in a ballet class. Since warm-up at the *barre* is key to preventing injury, five minutes (A) would not be sufficient to ensure dancers' bodies are warmed up enough to safely perform center work. B is incorrect because warm-up *barre* exercises should always be performed before center work to prevent injury. D is incorrect because spending a total of only ten minutes away from the *barre* would not provide adequate time for dancers to develop skill in movements that cannot be performed at the *barre*, such as jumps and turns.

92. D: The best approach in this case would be D, demonstrating versions of each exercise that are appropriate for the various levels. For example, a teacher could suggest that beginners do a *passé retiré*, intermediate students do a single *pirouette*, and advanced students do a double *pirouette*. If advanced students are ignored (A), they will not be challenged sufficiently to improve, and the approaches in both B and C may cause beginners to become injured, since they may attempt movements that are too difficult for them.

93. D: The best way to address technique problems is to address as many different learning styles as possible. Using imagery (A) appeals to auditory learners, demonstrating proper technique (B) appeals to visual learners, and manipulation (C) appeals to kinesthetic learners. By using as many of these methods as possible, all students will have a better chance of understanding the concept.

94. C: Body Mass Index (BMI) is helpful because it indicates whether a student's weight is proportional to his or her height. Since BMI is a ratio of height to weight, A is incorrect, and B is incorrect because BMI is not useful for converting between units of weight. Last, D is incorrect because BMI does not indicate the ratio of fat to muscle.

95. B: To make the combination described in Figure 3 more appropriate for technically advanced dancers, a teacher might change the *changements* to *entrechats*. Eliminating the *changements* (A) would make the combination marginally less difficult. Making the dancers do the combination twice (D) would increase the level of endurance required, but would not alter the technical difficulty. Last, asking dancers to execute the jumps in third position instead of fifth position (C) would also make the combination easier because it would reduce the amount of hip rotation.

96. A: In order to improve students' kinesthetic awareness and originality, a teacher might assign a contact improvisation exercise. This involves improvising movement while remaining in constant contact with another person or surface, and is the only exercise listed above that would promote both kinesthetic awareness and originality. The other three types of exercise might improve kinesthetic awareness to varying degrees, but do not involve developing original movements.

97. B: A written test would be an appropriate assessment tool for gauging students' ability to identify historical figures and their significance in dance history, since this involves factual knowledge. The other choices represent skills that could not be assessed effectively using a written assessment. First, such an assessment would probably not present an authentic stimulus for the skills in question, and second, it would provide only a single point of reference, while these skills are better assessed over time.

98. A: The best method for assessing this skill would be a written test supplemented by a performance-based assessment. Since this skill involves both a performance element ("perform dance phrases or dances from several time periods") and a factual element ("understanding of historical and social contexts"), a multi-faceted assessment would be necessary. The other assessment choices listed above only address one aspect of this skill.

99. C: Rubrics are most effective for assessing complex assignments. Rubrics set out specific criteria for student grading and may break a complex assignment into several specific areas in which different grades may be assigned. (For example, a student could receive separate grades for execution, stage presence and musicality, and originality of choreography.). Rubrics do not encourage students to analyze their thought processes, so they do not improve metacognitive skills (A). Typically they do not reference goal setting (B), and since a rubric is an assessment tool, not an assignment, it would not be helpful in teaching critical thinking (D).

100. D: The best way to assess students' ability to "demonstrate appropriate audience behavior and etiquette in the classroom and at performances" would be to explain appropriate audience behavior, and then take students to a performance and evaluate their behavior there. Asking students to choreograph and present a performance to friends and family (A) would not provide an opportunity for students to demonstrate appropriate behavior. Giving a test (C) would be the next best alternative if attending a real performance were not feasible, but it would not give students a chance to actively demonstrate the skill. Discussing appropriate audience behavior (B) is a pedagogical (teaching) method, not an assessment method.

How to Overcome Test Anxiety

Just the thought of taking a test is enough to make most people a little nervous. A test is an important event that can have a long-term impact on your future, so it's important to take it seriously and it's natural to feel anxious about performing well. But just because anxiety is normal, that doesn't mean that it's helpful in test taking, or that you should simply accept it as part of your life. Anxiety can have a variety of effects. These effects can be mild, like making you feel slightly nervous, or severe, like blocking your ability to focus or remember even a simple detail.

If you experience test anxiety—whether severe or mild—it's important to know how to beat it. To discover this, first you need to understand what causes test anxiety.

Causes of Test Anxiety

While we often think of anxiety as an uncontrollable emotional state, it can actually be caused by simple, practical things. One of the most common causes of test anxiety is that a person does not feel adequately prepared for their test. This feeling can be the result of many different issues such as poor study habits or lack of organization, but the most common culprit is time management. Starting to study too late, failing to organize your study time to cover all of the material, or being distracted while you study will mean that you're not well prepared for the test. This may lead to cramming the night before, which will cause you to be physically and mentally exhausted for the test. Poor time management also contributes to feelings of stress, fear, and hopelessness as you realize you are not well prepared but don't know what to do about it.

Other times, test anxiety is not related to your preparation for the test but comes from unresolved fear. This may be a past failure on a test, or poor performance on tests in general. It may come from comparing yourself to others who seem to be performing better or from the stress of living up to expectations. Anxiety may be driven by fears of the future—how failure on this test would affect your educational and career goals. These fears are often completely irrational, but they can still negatively impact your test performance.

Elements of Test Anxiety

As mentioned earlier, test anxiety is considered to be an emotional state, but it has physical and mental components as well. Sometimes you may not even realize that you are suffering from test anxiety until you notice the physical symptoms. These can include trembling hands, rapid heartbeat, sweating, nausea, and tense muscles. Extreme anxiety may lead to fainting or vomiting. Obviously, any of these symptoms can have a negative impact on testing. It is important to recognize them as soon as they begin to occur so that you can address the problem before it damages your performance.

The mental components of test anxiety include trouble focusing and inability to remember learned information. During a test, your mind is on high alert, which can help you recall information and stay focused for an extended period of time. However, anxiety interferes with your mind's natural processes, causing you to blank out, even on the questions you know well. The strain of testing during anxiety makes it difficult to stay focused, especially on a test that may take several hours. Extreme anxiety can take a huge mental toll, making it difficult not only to recall test information but even to understand the test questions or pull your thoughts together.

Effects of Test Anxiety

Test anxiety is like a disease—if left untreated, it will get progressively worse. Anxiety leads to poor performance, and this reinforces the feelings of fear and failure, which in turn lead to poor performances on subsequent tests. It can grow from a mild nervousness to a crippling condition. If allowed to progress, test anxiety can have a big impact on your schooling, and consequently on your future.

Test anxiety can spread to other parts of your life. Anxiety on tests can become anxiety in any stressful situation, and blanking on a test can turn into panicking in a job situation. But fortunately, you don't have to let anxiety rule your testing and determine your grades. There are a number of relatively simple steps you can take to move past anxiety and function normally on a test and in the rest of life.

Physical Steps for Beating Test Anxiety

While test anxiety is a serious problem, the good news is that it can be overcome. It doesn't have to control your ability to think and remember information. While it may take time, you can begin taking steps today to beat anxiety.

Just as your first hint that you may be struggling with anxiety comes from the physical symptoms, the first step to treating it is also physical. Rest is crucial for having a clear, strong mind. If you are tired, it is much easier to give in to anxiety. But if you establish good sleep habits, your body and mind will be ready to perform optimally, without the strain of exhaustion. Additionally, sleeping well helps you to retain information better, so you're more likely to recall the answers when you see the test questions.

Getting good sleep means more than going to bed on time. It's important to allow your brain time to relax. Take study breaks from time to time so it doesn't get overworked, and don't study right before bed. Take time to rest your mind before trying to rest your body, or you may find it difficult to fall asleep.

Along with sleep, other aspects of physical health are important in preparing for a test. Good nutrition is vital for good brain function. Sugary foods and drinks may give a burst of energy but this burst is followed by a crash, both physically and emotionally. Instead, fuel your body with protein and vitamin-rich foods.

Also, drink plenty of water. Dehydration can lead to headaches and exhaustion, especially if your brain is already under stress from the rigors of the test. Particularly if your test is a long one, drink water during the breaks. And if possible, take an energy-boosting snack to eat between sections.

Along with sleep and diet, a third important part of physical health is exercise. Maintaining a steady workout schedule is helpful, but even taking 5-minute study breaks to walk can help get your blood pumping faster and clear your head. Exercise also releases endorphins, which contribute to a positive feeling and can help combat test anxiety.

When you nurture your physical health, you are also contributing to your mental health. If your body is healthy, your mind is much more likely to be healthy as well. So take time to rest, nourish your body with healthy food and water, and get moving as much as possible. Taking these physical steps will make you stronger and more able to take the mental steps necessary to overcome test anxiety.

Mental Steps for Beating Test Anxiety

Working on the mental side of test anxiety can be more challenging, but as with the physical side, there are clear steps you can take to overcome it. As mentioned earlier, test anxiety often stems from lack of preparation, so the obvious solution is to prepare for the test. Effective studying may be the most important weapon you have for beating test anxiety, but you can and should employ several other mental tools to combat fear.

First, boost your confidence by reminding yourself of past success—tests or projects that you aced. If you're putting as much effort into preparing for this test as you did for those, there's no reason you should expect to fail here. Work hard to prepare; then trust your preparation.

Second, surround yourself with encouraging people. It can be helpful to find a study group, but be sure that the people you're around will encourage a positive attitude. If you spend time with others who are anxious or cynical, this will only contribute to your own anxiety. Look for others who are motivated to study hard from a desire to succeed, not from a fear of failure.

Third, reward yourself. A test is physically and mentally tiring, even without anxiety, and it can be helpful to have something to look forward to. Plan an activity following the test, regardless of the outcome, such as going to a movie or getting ice cream.

When you are taking the test, if you find yourself beginning to feel anxious, remind yourself that you know the material. Visualize successfully completing the test. Then take a few deep, relaxing breaths and return to it. Work through the questions carefully but with confidence, knowing that you are capable of succeeding.

Developing a healthy mental approach to test taking will also aid in other areas of life. Test anxiety affects more than just the actual test—it can be damaging to your mental health and even contribute to depression. It's important to beat test anxiety before it becomes a problem for more than testing.

Study Strategy

Being prepared for the test is necessary to combat anxiety, but what does being prepared look like? You may study for hours on end and still not feel prepared. What you need is a strategy for test prep. The next few pages outline our recommended steps to help you plan out and conquer the challenge of preparation.

Step 1: Scope Out the Test

Learn everything you can about the format (multiple choice, essay, etc.) and what will be on the test. Gather any study materials, course outlines, or sample exams that may be available. Not only will this help you to prepare, but knowing what to expect can help to alleviate test anxiety.

Step 2: Map Out the Material

Look through the textbook or study guide and make note of how many chapters or sections it has. Then divide these over the time you have. For example, if a book has 15 chapters and you have five days to study, you need to cover three chapters each day. Even better, if you have the time, leave an extra day at the end for overall review after you have gone through the material in depth.

If time is limited, you may need to prioritize the material. Look through it and make note of which sections you think you already have a good grasp on, and which need review. While you are studying, skim quickly through the familiar sections and take more time on the challenging parts.

Write out your plan so you don't get lost as you go. Having a written plan also helps you feel more in control of the study, so anxiety is less likely to arise from feeling overwhelmed at the amount to cover.

Step 3: Gather Your Tools

Decide what study method works best for you. Do you prefer to highlight in the book as you study and then go back over the highlighted portions? Or do you type out notes of the important information? Or is it helpful to make flashcards that you can carry with you? Assemble the pens, index cards, highlighters, post-it notes, and any other materials you may need so you won't be distracted by getting up to find things while you study.

If you're having a hard time retaining the information or organizing your notes, experiment with different methods. For example, try color-coding by subject with colored pens, highlighters, or post-it notes. If you learn better by hearing, try recording yourself reading your notes so you can listen while in the car, working out, or simply sitting at your desk. Ask a friend to quiz you from your flashcards, or try teaching someone the material to solidify it in your mind.

Step 4: Create Your Environment

It's important to avoid distractions while you study. This includes both the obvious distractions like visitors and the subtle distractions like an uncomfortable chair (or a too-comfortable couch that makes you want to fall asleep). Set up the best study environment possible: good lighting and a comfortable work area. If background music helps you focus, you may want to turn it on, but otherwise keep the room quiet. If you are using a computer to take notes, be sure you don't have any other windows open, especially applications like social media, games, or anything else that could distract you. Silence your phone and turn off notifications. Be sure to keep water close by so you stay hydrated while you study (but avoid unhealthy drinks and snacks).

Also, take into account the best time of day to study. Are you freshest first thing in the morning? Try to set aside some time then to work through the material. Is your mind clearer in the afternoon or evening? Schedule your study session then. Another method is to study at the same time of day that you will take the test, so that your brain gets used to working on the material at that time and will be ready to focus at test time.

Step 5: Study!

Once you have done all the study preparation, it's time to settle into the actual studying. Sit down, take a few moments to settle your mind so you can focus, and begin to follow your study plan. Don't give in to distractions or let yourself procrastinate. This is your time to prepare so you'll be ready to fearlessly approach the test. Make the most of the time and stay focused.

Of course, you don't want to burn out. If you study too long you may find that you're not retaining the information very well. Take regular study breaks. For example, taking five minutes out of every hour to walk briskly, breathing deeply and swinging your arms, can help your mind stay fresh.

As you get to the end of each chapter or section, it's a good idea to do a quick review. Remind yourself of what you learned and work on any difficult parts. When you feel that you've mastered the material, move on to the next part. At the end of your study session, briefly skim through your notes again.

But while review is helpful, cramming last minute is NOT. If at all possible, work ahead so that you won't need to fit all your study into the last day. Cramming overloads your brain with more information than it can process and retain, and your tired mind may struggle to recall even previously learned information when it is overwhelmed with last-minute study. Also, the urgent nature of cramming and the stress placed on your brain contribute to anxiety. You'll be more likely to go to the test feeling unprepared and having trouble thinking clearly.

So don't cram, and don't stay up late before the test, even just to review your notes at a leisurely pace. Your brain needs rest more than it needs to go over the information again. In fact, plan to finish your studies by noon or early afternoon the day before the test. Give your brain the rest of the day to relax or focus on other things, and get a good night's sleep. Then you will be fresh for the test and better able to recall what you've studied.

Step 6: Take a Practice Test

Many courses offer sample tests, either online or in the study materials. This is an excellent resource to check whether you have mastered the material, as well as to prepare for the test format and environment.

Check the test format ahead of time: the number of questions, the type (multiple choice, free response, etc.), and the time limit. Then create a plan for working through them. For example, if you have 30 minutes to take a 60-question test, your limit is 30 seconds per question. Spend less time on the questions you know well so that you can take more time on the difficult ones.

If you have time to take several practice tests, take the first one open book, with no time limit. Work through the questions at your own pace and make sure you fully understand them. Gradually work up to taking a test under test conditions: sit at a desk with all study materials put away and set a timer. Pace yourself to make sure you finish the test with time to spare and go back to check your answers if you have time.

After each test, check your answers. On the questions you missed, be sure you understand why you missed them. Did you misread the question (tests can use tricky wording)? Did you forget the information? Or was it something you hadn't learned? Go back and study any shaky areas that the practice tests reveal.

Taking these tests not only helps with your grade, but also aids in combating test anxiety. If you're already used to the test conditions, you're less likely to worry about it, and working through tests until you're scoring well gives you a confidence boost. Go through the practice tests until you feel comfortable, and then you can go into the test knowing that you're ready for it.

Test Tips

On test day, you should be confident, knowing that you've prepared well and are ready to answer the questions. But aside from preparation, there are several test day strategies you can employ to maximize your performance.

First, as stated before, get a good night's sleep the night before the test (and for several nights before that, if possible). Go into the test with a fresh, alert mind rather than staying up late to study.

Try not to change too much about your normal routine on the day of the test. It's important to eat a nutritious breakfast, but if you normally don't eat breakfast at all, consider eating just a protein bar. If you're a coffee drinker, go ahead and have your normal coffee. Just make sure you time it so that the caffeine doesn't wear off right in the middle of your test. Avoid sugary beverages, and drink enough water to stay hydrated but not so much that you need a restroom break 10 minutes into the test. If your test isn't first thing in the morning, consider going for a walk or doing a light workout before the test to get your blood flowing.

Allow yourself enough time to get ready, and leave for the test with plenty of time to spare so you won't have the anxiety of scrambling to arrive in time. Another reason to be early is to select a good seat. It's helpful to sit away from doors and windows, which can be distracting. Find a good seat, get out your supplies, and settle your mind before the test begins.

When the test begins, start by going over the instructions carefully, even if you already know what to expect. Make sure you avoid any careless mistakes by following the directions.

Then begin working through the questions, pacing yourself as you've practiced. If you're not sure on an answer, don't spend too much time on it, and don't let it shake your confidence. Either skip it and come back later, or eliminate as many wrong answers as possible and guess among the remaining ones. Don't dwell on these questions as you continue—put them out of your mind and focus on what lies ahead.

Be sure to read all of the answer choices, even if you're sure the first one is the right answer. Sometimes you'll find a better one if you keep reading. But don't second-guess yourself if you do immediately know the answer. Your gut instinct is usually right. Don't let test anxiety rob you of the information you know.

If you have time at the end of the test (and if the test format allows), go back and review your answers. Be cautious about changing any, since your first instinct tends to be correct, but make sure you didn't misread any of the questions or accidentally mark the wrong answer choice. Look over any you skipped and make an educated guess.

At the end, leave the test feeling confident. You've done your best, so don't waste time worrying about your performance or wishing you could change anything. Instead, celebrate the successful completion of this test. And finally, use this test to learn how to deal with anxiety even better next time.

Review Video: Test Anxiety
Visit mometrix.com/academy and enter code: 100340

Important Qualification

Not all anxiety is created equal. If your test anxiety is causing major issues in your life beyond the classroom or testing center, or if you are experiencing troubling physical symptoms related to your anxiety, it may be a sign of a serious physiological or psychological condition. If this sounds like your situation, we strongly encourage you to seek professional help.

Online Resources

Due to our efforts to try to keep this book to a manageable length, we've created a link that will give you access to all of your online resources:

mometrix.com/resources719/aepadance

It's Your Moment, Let's Celebrate It!

Share your story @mometrixtestpreparation